GET READY FOR GRADE **4** TEACHER RECOMMENDED

Kids

SUMMER

ACADEMY

ARGOPREP

7 DAYS A WEEK

8 WEEKS

- Mathematics
- English
- Science
- Reading
- Writing
- Experiments
- Mazes
- Puzzles
- Fitness

GRADE 3-4

ArgoPrep is one of the leading providers of supplemental educational products and services. We offer affordable and effective test prep solutions to educators, parents and students. Learning should be fun and easy! To access more resources visit us at www.argoprep.com.

Our goal is to make your life easier, so let us know how we can help you by e-mailing us at: info@argoprep.com.

- ArgoPrep is a recipient of the prestigious **Mom's Choice Award**.
- ArgoPrep also received the 2019 **Seal of Approval** from Homeschool.com for our award-winning workbooks.
- ArgoPrep was awarded the 2019 **National Parenting Products Award, Gold Medal Parent's Choice Award** and **the Tillywig Brain Child Award.**

TABLE OF CONTENTS

TABLE OF CONTENTS

TABLE OF CONTENTS

FIRESTORM
WARRIOR

Completed your summer journey?
Craving more insights? Follow the link
provided or simply scan the QR code to
access exclusive **BONUS** materials!

argoprep.com/summer4

KIDS SUMMER ACADEMY SERIES

ArgoPrep's **Kids Summer Academy** series helps prevent summer learning loss and gets students ready for their new school year by reinforcing core foundations in math, english and science. Our workbooks also introduce new concepts so students can get a head start and be on top of their game for the new school year!

WATER FIRE

DANCE HERO

ADRASTOS THE SUPER WARRIOR

MYSTICAL NINJA

GREEN POISON

RAPID NINJA

CAPTAIN ARGO

THUNDER WARRIOR

CAPTAIN BRAVERY

FIRESTORM WARRIOR

Give your character a name

Write down the special ability or powers your character has and how you will help your community with the powers.

Great! You are all set. To become an incredible hero, we need to strengthen our skills in **English, math,** and **science**. Let's get started.

Are you ready to start your journey?
Let's dive right into week 1.

WEEK 1

Did you know our oceans cover more than 70 percent of the Earth's surface?

It's also estimated that roughly 70% of the oxygen we breathe is produced by the ocean from marine plants. How cool is that!

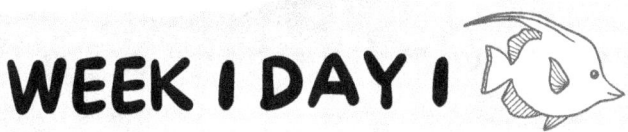
As your vocabulary grows, it's important to understand how to express ideas using a variety of different words. One way writers do this, is by adding certain beginnings or endings to words that change or deepen their meaning. It's important that you know how to attach prefixes and suffixes to words for your own writing, but it's equally important to be able to identify and define them as you read.

Key Terms

Root Word: a basic word that you would use in a sentence

Prefix: letters added <u>before</u> the beginning of a root word to change or add to the meaning

 ## For Example...

Root Word: Happy (joyful or content)
Prefix: Un- (meaning "not")
New Word: Unhappy (meaning "<u>not</u> joyful or content")

In a sentence: My sister was <u>unhappy</u> that the tooth fairy only left her a nickel.

Root Word: Sentence (a complete thought expressed in words)
Prefix: Mid (meaning "in the middle of")
New Word: Mid-sentence (meaning "in the middle of a sentence")

In a sentence: I get frustrated when people interrupt me <u>mid-sentence.</u>

Common Prefixes

Prefix	Definition	Example
Anti-	Fighting against	Antibacterial (fighting against bacteria) Antiaging (fighting the aging process)
Auto-	To one's self	Autobiography (a book about yourself) Automatic (working by itself)
De-	To cancel out, reverse, or remove	Debug (to remove bugs or glitches from software) Destruct (to reverse the process of something being constructed)

WEEK 1 DAY 1  OVERVIEW OF ENGLISH CONCEPTS
PREFIXES

Prefix	Definition	Example
Mid-	In the middle of	Mid-year (in the middle of the year) Midfield (in the middle of the field)
Mis-	Done badly or incorrectly	Mislead (to lead people in the wrong direction) Miscalculate (to do math wrong)
Pre-	Before	Prewar (before the war) Prejudge (to judge before having the facts)
Post-	After	Postwar (after the war) Postseason (the part of the sports schedule after the main season)
Re-	Again	Rediscover (to find something again) Redo (to do again or do over)
Trans-	Across or Change	Transatlantic (across the Atlantic Ocean) Transform (changing something's form or appearance)
Un-	Not	Unhappy (not happy) Undo (reverse something that was done)

The Hare With Many Friends
By Aesop

A Hare was very popular with the other beasts who all claimed to be her friends. But one day she heard the hounds approaching and hoped to escape them by the aid of her many Friends. So, she went to the horse, and asked him to carry her away from the hounds on his back. But he declined, stating that he had important work to do for his master. "I feel sure," he said, "that all your other friends will come to your assistance."

She then applied to the bull, and hoped that he would repel the hounds with his horns. The bull replied: "I am very sorry, but I have an appointment with a lady; but I feel sure that our friend the goat will do what you want."

The goat, however, feared that his back might do her some harm if he took her upon it. The ram, he felt sure, was the proper friend to apply to. So she went to the ram and told him the case. The ram replied: "Another time, my dear friend. I do not like to interfere on the present occasion, as hounds have been known to eat sheep as well as hares."

The Hare then applied, as a last hope, to the calf, who regretted that he was unable to help her, as he did not like to take the responsibility upon himself, as so many older persons than himself had declined the task. By this time the hounds were quite near, and the Hare took to her heels and luckily escaped.

He that has many friends, has no friends.

I. Why is the Hare seeking help from her friends?

2. Why is the phrase "who all claimed to be" in the first sentence important to the rest of the story?

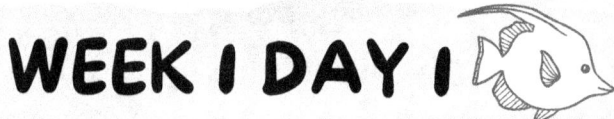
3. Which animal tries to convince the Hare that it will actually hurt them if they try to help her?

    A. The horse
    B. The bull
    C. The goat
    D. The calf

4. Which of these phrases from the passage contains a **prefix**?

    A. The horse was sure "all your other friends will come"
    B. The bull said he "had an appointment with a lady"
    C. The ram is concerned that "hounds have been known to eat sheep as well as hares"
    D. The calf said "he was unable to help her"

5. How does the Hare's story connect to the author's point: "He that has many friends, has no friends"?

WEEK 1 DAY 1

Identifying and Defining Words with Prefixes

Directions:

Circle the word in each sentence that uses a prefix. Then, on the line below, write a short definition for that word based on your understanding of the prefix.

1. Saturday's soccer game was very frustrating because the referees appeared to be completely untrained.

   ~~~~~~

2. The printer got completely jammed up because I misaligned the paper when I filled it.

   ~~~~~~

3. Mr. Francis allows students to retake his quizzes if they score below a 75%.

   ~~~~~~

4. The autocorrect function on cell phones and word processing programs cannot always be trusted.

   ~~~~~~

5. If a web page is not loading correctly, it can be useful to hit the refresh button and allow the process to start over.

FITNESS

Please be aware of your environment and be safe at all times. If you cannot do an exercise, just try your best.

1 - Abs: 3 times   Repeat these **exercises 3 ROUNDS**

2 - Lunges: 2 times to each leg.
Note: Use your body weight or books as weight to do leg lunges.

4 - Run: 50m
Note: Run 25 meters to one side and 25 meters back to the starting position.

3 - Plank: 6 sec.

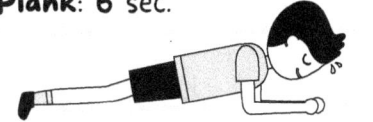

Saving the Birds
By James Baldwin

One day in spring four men were riding on horseback along a country road. These men were lawyers, and they were going to the next town to attend court. There had been a rain, and the ground was very soft. Water was dripping from the trees, and the grass was wet. The four lawyers rode along, one behind another; for the pathway was narrow, and the mud on each side of it was deep. They rode slowly, and talked and laughed and were very jolly.

As they were passing through a grove of small trees, they heard a great fluttering over their heads and a feeble chirping in the grass by the roadside.

"Stith! stith! stith!" came from the leafy branches above them.

"Cheep! cheep! cheep!" came from the wet grass.

"What is the matter here?" asked the first lawyer, whose name was Speed. "Oh, it's only some old robins!" said the second lawyer, whose name was Hardin. "The storm has blown two of the little ones out of the nest. They are too young to fly, and the mother bird is making a great fuss about it."

"What a pity! They'll die down there in the grass," said the third lawyer, whose name I forget.

"Oh, well! They're nothing but birds," said Mr. Hardin. "Why should we bother?"

"Yes, why should we?" said Mr. Speed.

The three men, as they passed, looked down and saw the little birds fluttering in the cold, wet grass. They saw the mother robin flying about, and crying to her mate.

Then they rode on, talking and laughing as before. In a few minutes they had forgotten about the birds.

But the fourth lawyer, whose name was Abraham Lincoln, stopped. He got down from his horse and very gently took the little ones up in his big warm hands.

They did not seem frightened, but chirped softly, as if they knew they were safe.

"Never mind, my little fellows," said Mr. Lincoln "I will put you in your own cozy little bed."

Then he looked up to find the nest from which they had fallen. It was high, much higher than he could reach.

But Mr. Lincoln could climb. He had climbed many a tree when he was a boy. He put the birds softly, one by one, into their warm little home. Two other baby birds were there, that had not fallen out. All cuddled down together and were very happy.

Soon the three lawyers who had ridden ahead stopped at a spring to give their horses water.

"Where is Lincoln?" asked one.

All were surprised to find that he was not with them.

"Do you remember those birds?" said Mr. Speed. "Very likely he has stopped to take care of them."

In a few minutes Mr. Lincoln joined them. His shoes were covered with mud; he had torn his coat on the thorny tree.

"Hello, Abraham!" said Mr. Hardin. "Where have you been?"

"I stopped a minute to give those birds to their mother," he answered.

"Well, we always thought you were a hero," said Mr. Speed. "Now we know it."

Then all three of them laughed heartily. They thought it so foolish that a strong man should take so much trouble just for some worthless young birds.

"Gentlemen," said Mr. Lincoln, "I could not have slept to-night, if I had left those helpless little robins to perish in the wet grass."

Abraham Lincoln afterwards became very famous as a lawyer and statesman. He was elected president. Next to Washington he was the greatest American.

1. How is Abraham Lincoln different from the other characters in the passage?

2. Which of these words with a prefix describes the three other lawyers traveling with Lincoln?

    A. Misunderstanding
    B. Unhelpful
    C. Anti-bird
    D. Post-travels

3. Which event in the story shows that Abraham Lincoln was willing to help others, even when it was inconvenient for him?

4. How do the other lawyers feel about Abraham Lincoln?

5. How do you know that the author of the passage admired Abraham Lincoln a great deal?

ACTIVITIES
PREFIXES

Directions:

Fill in the blank by adding one of the <u>Common Prefixes</u> to the word in parentheses at the end of the sentence. Be sure to reread the sentence with your new word in place to make sure it makes sense!

1. Maria's nail polish cracked while she was working in the science lab, so she had to _____ it. (APPLY)

2. Most commercial airlines use an _____ system, which means the cockpit crew can focus most of their time planning routes and communicating with air traffic control instead of flying the plane. (PILOT)

3. Even though Mark is a nice guy, I find him _____ because he can't keep a secret. (TRUSTWORTHY)

4. Before computers and copy machines, people had to _____ books by hand, which meant copying every last word onto new pieces of paper. (SCRIBE)

5. Many people use _____ techniques to help them relax and forget about their troubles. (STRESS)

FITNESS

Please be aware of your environment and be safe at all times. If you cannot do an exercise, just try your best.

Repeat these **exercises 3 ROUNDS**

2 - Side Bending: 5 times to each side. Note: try to touch your feet.

1 - Squats: 5 times. Note: imagine you are trying to sit on a chair.

3 - Tree Pose: Stay as long as possible. Note: do the same with the other leg.

WEEK 1 DAY 3  MATH

Addition Practice Questions

1. What is the sum of 246 and 352?

   A. 568
   B. 598
   C. 618
   D. 628

2. Which addition sentence equals to 1,025?

   A. 457 + 568
   B. 563 + 492
   C. 371 + 634
   D. 496 + 589

3. What is 564 added to 126?

   Answer _____

4. What is 289 + 325?

   Answer _____

5. What is the sum of 45, 28 and 31?

   A. 98
   B. 104
   C. 112
   D. 114

6. What is the missing number in this equation?

   $$78 + \_\_\_\_\_ = 891$$

   A. 793
   B. 803
   C. 813
   D. 823

7. What is the sum of 289, 103 and 461?

   Answer _____

8. What is the sum of 765 and 341?

   Answer _____

9. Which equation is true?

   A. 347 + 168 = 505
   B. 684 + 127 = 821
   C. 373 + 548 = 911
   D. 467 + 473 = 940

10. Which equation is FALSE?

   A. 652 + 387 = 1,039
   B. 448 + 551 = 1,009
   C. 574 + 458 = 1,032
   D. 345 + 695 = 1,040

Subtraction Practice Questions

1. What is the difference between 857 and 324?

   A. 543
   B. 533
   C. 532
   D. 523

2. What is 568 subtracted from 1,120?

   Answer _____

3. What is the missing number in this equation?
   $$787 - _____ = 304$$

   Answer _____

4. Choose the expression that is true.

   A. 1,368 - 124 = 1,244
   B. 1,257 - 1,136 = 125
   C. 786 - 541 = 255
   D. 689 - 352 = 347

5. What is 975 - 346 - 154?

   Answer _____

20

6. Choose the option that has a value less than the difference between **637** and **358**.

   A. 289
   B. 269
   C. 299
   D. 309

7. Which expression is FALSE?

   A. 562 - 397 = 165
   B. 473 - 189 = 284
   C. 735 - 697 = 48
   D. 464 - 277 = 187

8. Which expression is true?

   A. 638 - 285 = 363
   B. 864 - 783 = 81
   C. 591 - 386 = 215
   D. 748 - 359 = 379

9. What is 834 - 562?

   Answer _____

10. What is **347** subtracted from **1,007**?

    Answer _____

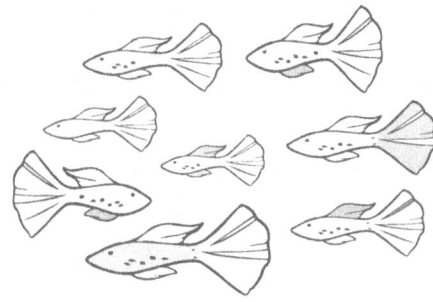

FITNESS

Repeat these
exercises
3 ROUNDS

Please be aware of your environment and be safe at all times. If you cannot do an exercise, just try your best.

1 - Bend forward: 10 times.
Note: try to touch your feet. Make sure to keep your back straight and if needed you can bend your knees.

2 - Lunges: 3 times to each leg.
Note: Use your body weight or books as weight to do leg lunges.

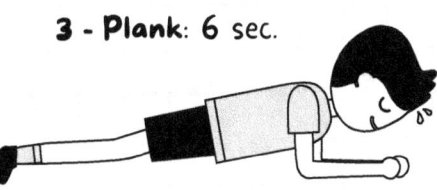

3 - Plank: 6 sec.

4 - Abs: 10 times

Multiplication Practice Questions

1. What is 8 × 30?

   A. 240
   B. 830
   C. 24
   D. 83

2. Choose a pair of numbers that results in a product of 560?

   A. 7 and 8
   B. 70 and 80
   C. 70 and 8
   D. 700 and 800

3. Which expression best represents the picture below?

   A. 9 + 5
   B. 9 + 9 + 9 + 9 + 9
   C. 5 + 5 + 5 + 5 + 5 + 5 + 5 + 5 + 5
   D. 9 + 5 + 5 + 5 + 5

4. Which picture represents 6 × 8?

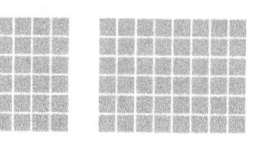  

   1   2   3   4

   A. 1
   B. 2
   C. 3
   D. 4

5. Which expression is true?

   A. 7 + 7 + 7 + 7 = 7 + 4
   B. 8 + 8 + 8 + 4 = 8 × 4
   C. 20 + 20 + 20 = 20 × 3
   D. 5 + 5 + 5 + 40 = 5 × 40

6. Write a multiplication expression which is represented by the model below?

   Answer _____

7. What is the missing number in this equation?

   $$80 \times \text{\_\_\_\_} = 320$$

   Answer _____

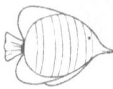

8. Which expression is the same as $(30 \times 4) + (6 \times 4)$?

    A. $30 + 6 \times 4$
    B. 36×4
    C. $30 \times 4 + 6$
    D. $30 \times (4 + 6)$

9. What is 4×26?

    Answer _____

10. Find 70×9.

    Answer _____

Division Practice Questions

1. Which expression best represents the picture below?

    A. $5 \div 3$
    B. $15 \div 5$
    C. $5 \div 15$
    D. $3 \div 5$

Repeat these exercises 3 ROUNDS

Please be aware of your environment and be safe at all times. If you cannot do an exercise, just try your best.

1 - High Plank: 6 sec.

2 - Chair: 10 sec.
Note: sit on an imaginary chair, keep your back straight.

3 - Waist Hooping: 10 times. Note: if you do not have a hoop, pretend you have an imaginary hoop and rotate your hips 10 times.

4 - Abs: 10 times

Division Practice Questions

1. Which equation could be represented by the picture below?

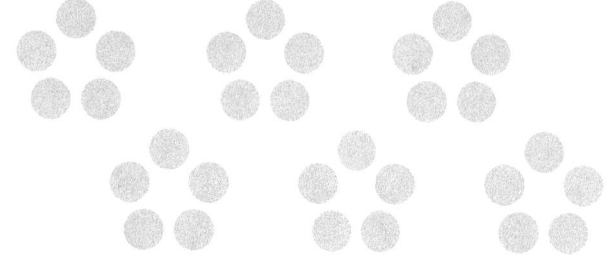

A. $30 \div 5 = 5$
B. $5 \div 30 = 6$
C. $30 \div 6 = 5$
D. $30 \div 6 = 6$

2. What is $480 \div 6$?

Answer _____

3. What is the quotient when 99 is divided by 9?

Answer _____

4. Choose the number sentence below that has a quotient of 60.

A. $540 \div 9$
B. $640 \div 8$
C. $320 \div 4$
D. $480 \div 6$

5. Which number sentence below is FALSE?

A. $240 \div 8 = 30$
B. $84 \div 4 = 80 \div 4 + 4 \div 4$
C. $56 \div 8 = 56 \div 7$
D. $45 \div 5 = (40 + 5) \div 5$

6. Find the divider of 810 to get 90.

Answer _____

7. What is the missing number in the equation $48 \div \_\_\_\_\_ = 12$?

Answer _____

8. What is the missing number in the equation $\_\_\_ \div 24 = 5$?

Answer _____

9. How many times is the number 270 greater than the number 3?

Answer _____

Word problems: Mix of add/subtract/multiply/divide

1. Charlie has 3 books with 285 pages in each book. How many pages are there in total for the three books?

A. 825
B. 855
C. 865
D. 885

2. Mr. Anderson has 8 students and he gave each of them 4 word problems. Which expression represents how to find the number of word problems he gave out altogether?

A. $4 + 8$
B. $8 + 8 + 8$
C. $4 + 4 + 4 + 4 + 4 + 4 + 4 + 4$
D. $4 + 4 + 4 + 4 + 4 + 4$

3. Mark has 8 brownies and 9 cakes in each box. If he has 7 boxes, how many brownies and cakes does he have altogether?

A. 119
B. 107
C. 131
D. 98

4. Cara bought **320** cookies. She had to put them into **8** boxes. How many cookies did Cara put into each box?

   A. 44
   B. 30
   C. 40
   D. 36

5. Grace scored **96** points, which was **3** times more than Carter. How many points did Carter score?

   A. 31
   B. 32
   C. 33
   D. 34

6. Wyatt collected **23** fewer toy cars than Michael. If Michael collected **75** toy cars, how many toy cars did Wyatt collect?

   Answer _____

7. Scarlett wants to buy a $340 phone. She has saved $100 and thinks she can save $60 per month. How many months will it take her to save enough money to buy the phone?

   Answer _____

8. If Mr. Miller split **72** pencils among 12 students, how many pencils did each student receive?

   Answer _____

9. There are 135 potato plants and 148 cucumber plants. How many plants are there in all?

   Answer _____

10. Hans had 1,126 yellow stars. If he gave 214 to his sister, how many stars did Hans have left?

    Answer _____

Please be aware of your environment and be safe at all times. If you cannot do an exercise, just try your best.

2 - Bend Down: 10 sec.

3 - Chair: 10 sec.

1 - Down Dog: 10 sec.

4 - Child Pose: 20 sec.

5 - Shavasana: as long as you can. Note: think of happy moments and relax your mind.

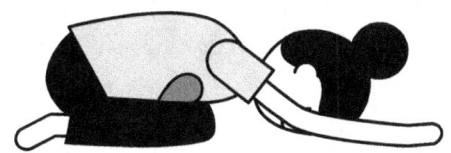

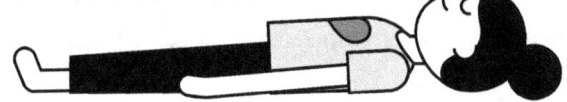

WEEK 1 DAY 6 EXPERIMENT

Comparing Mass by Making a Balance

All objects have **mass**. Mass is a measurement of **how much** material something is made out of. Mass is different than weight because mass is constant, while weight is partially determined by the force of gravity. (For example, your weight would be different on the Moon than it is on Earth because of the differences in gravity, but your mass would be the same!)

A **balance** is a device that scientists use to measure or compare masses. Today, we'll be making a balance that you can use to compare the masses of different household objects.

Materials:

- Plastic Coat Hanger
- Yarn, string, or twine (about 4-5 feet total)
- A tape measure or ruler
- Scissors
- Hole Punch (optional)
- Assorted small household objects (must fit into one of the cups!)

Procedure:

1. Using the hole punch (or scissors, if you don't have one), make two holes just below the rim and directly across from each other in each of the cups, so that the cups can be hung by the string.

2. Using your tape measure or ruler and scissors, cut your length of yarn, string, or twine exactly in half.

3. Feed the lengths of string or yarn through the holes you just created in the cup, so that, when you hold the loose ends of the string, the cup is hanging downward with the opening facing up.

4. Tie the loose ends of the lengths of string to the bottom corners of the hanger. One cup should be hanging from the bottom-left corner of the hanger, while the other should be hanging from the bottom-right corner. Make sure the knots are tied so that the two cups are hanging down at the same length. This is important to make sure your balance works accurately!

5. Hook the top of the hanger onto a safe place where both cups can dangle downward.

6. Choose two of the small household objects you gathered and place each of them in one of the cups. One of the cups should hang down lower than the other. This means that the object in that cup has a greater mass!

7. Using your balance and some note paper, compare all the objects you gathered to one another and rank them from highest mass to lowest mass

8. When you're done with this activity, be sure to save your balance because we'll be using it in future experiments as well.

Follow-Up Questions:

1. Why do you think it was important that the lengths of string or yarn were the same?

2. What was the most massive object you put in your balance?

Please be aware of your environment and be safe at all times. If you cannot do an exercise, just try your best.

1 - Tree Pose: Stay as long as possible. Note: do on one leg then on another.

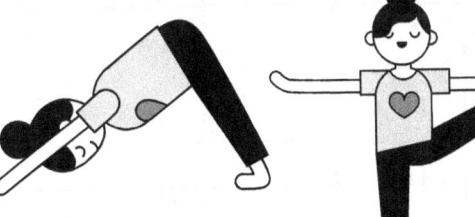

2 - Down Dog: 10 sec.

3 - Stretching: Stay as long as possible. Note: do on one leg then on another.

6 - Shavasana: 5 min. Note: this pose is very important and provides you with long term benefits. Try not to skip this. Close your eyes and imagine who you want to be and what your goals are! Always think happy thoughts.

5 - Book Pose: 6 sec. Note: Keep your core tight. Legs should be across from your eyes.

4 - Lower Plank: 6 sec. Note: Keep your back straight and body tight.

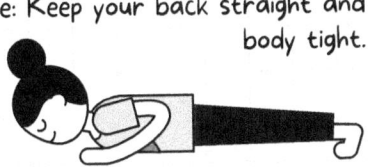

WEEK 1 DAY 7 MAZE

Task: Help find the way home for these lost tourists.
Color in the path they need to take.

Oh yeah!
Looks like you are getting the hang of this. Excited for week 2? I know I sure am!

WEEK 2

Did you know humans have only explored about 5% of the ocean?

There are so many things we do not yet know about our oceans. As we continue to research and improve our technology, we will learn more fascinating facts about our oceans.

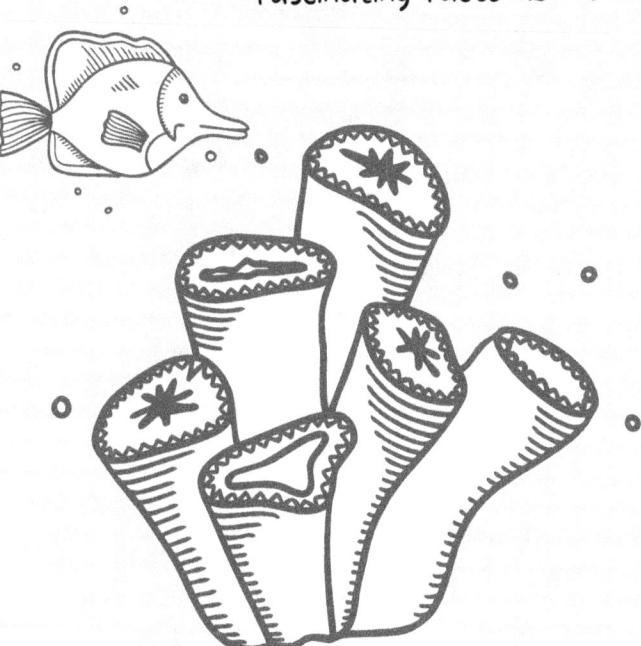

 Key Terms

Root Word: a basic word that you would use in a sentence

Prefix: letters added before the beginning of a root word to change or add to the meaning

Suffix: letters added after the end of a root word to change or add to the meaning

For Example...

Root Word: Teach (to communicate information or skills to)

Suffix: -able (meaning "capable of being")

New Word: Teachable (meaning "capable of being taught")

In a sentence: I don't know a lot about suffixes yet, but I am very teachable.

Common Suffixes

Suffix	Definition	Example
-able/-ible	Able to do something	Drinkable (able to be drunk safely) Flexible (able to flex or bend)
-dom	A situation built around a single idea	Kingdom (a situation in which a king is in charge) Boredom (a situation in which being bored is the main feeling)
-ee	Someone receiving something	Employee (someone receiving employment) Trainee (someone receiving training)
-er/-or	Someone who does something	Swimmer (someone who swims) Creator (someone who creates things)
-ful	Being filled with a certain characteristic	Helpful (filled with the desire to help others) Beautiful (filled with beauty)

WEEK 2 DAY 1  OVERVIEW OF ENGLISH CONCEPTS SUFFIXES

Suffix	Definition	Example
-ing	Turns a standard verb into a verbal adjective to describe the present action of the noun	Swimming (the thing you do with your arms and legs in water) Eating (the thing you do at meal time)
-ism	A philosophy or belief system	Traditionalism (the philosophy that old traditions are the best) Buddhism (belief in the philosophy of Buddha)
-ist	A follower of a philosophy or belief system	Traditionalist (someone who believes that old traditions are the best) Buddhist (someone who believes in the philosophy of Buddha)
-less	Without	Homeless (without a home) Friendless (without a friend)
-ness	Turns a descriptive word (adjective) into a thing (noun)	Softness (the feeling that soft things have) Happiness (the feeling of being joyful or content)

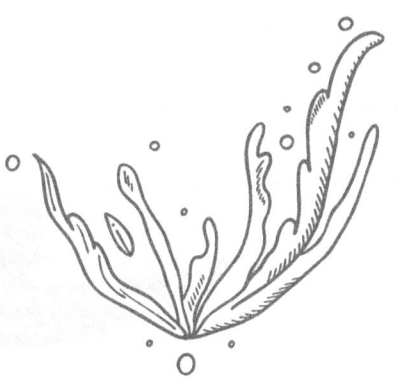

The Town Mouse and The Country Mouse
By Aesop

There were once two mice: one who lived in a town, and one who lived out in the country. They were close friends from when they were young, but they led very different lives as adult mice because of their different situations. One year, the Country Mouse invited the Town Mouse to come visit him for a week to catch up and learn more about the freedom of country life.

The Country Mouse showed the Town Mouse how to eat roots and cornstalks that were left in the field, but the Town Mouse didn't enjoy the experience at all. "Out here in the country, you live like an ant!" he told his friend. "It's so hard for you to find food, and then the food you find is plain and dusty. In the town, there's tons of delicious food, and the people make it easy to get to."

The Country Mouse couldn't deny that the town seemed much more convenient, so he followed the Town Mouse back to his home. The Town Mouse showed him how to move from one kitchen to the next through the walls of an apartment building, collecting vegetables, beans, bread, and even honey. The Country Mouse was extremely impressed with how easy it had been to find food and thought that maybe he should move to the town as well.

Once the two mice had assembled a feast, they sat down in one of the kitchens to eat it. However, just as they were about to take a bite, a human opened the front door of the apartment, which scared them so bad they had to run back into the walls. After a few minutes of waiting for the person to pass, the two mice returned to the kitchen.

Just as they were about to eat again, the human walked into the kitchen to grab a teacup and screamed at the sight of the two mice. Terrified, the Town Mouse and Country Mouse both retreated into the walls.

"I'm going back home," the hungry Country Mouse told his friend with a frown. "I agree that the food here is outstanding, but is far too dangerous to appreciate!"

1. According to the Town Mouse, why is life in town better than life in the country?

_____

_____

2. How does the Country Mouse's experience of the town differ from that of the Town Mouse?

~~~~~~

~~~~~~

~~~~~~

3. Which of these words from the first paragraph uses a suffix to add meaning?

   A. Mice
   B. Town
   C. Lives
   D. Freedom

4. Which of these words from the passage uses the suffix "-ing" to turn an action (verb) into a verbal adjective?

   A. Collecting (Paragraph 3)
   B. Waiting (Paragraph 4)
   C. Building (Paragraph 3)
   D. Outstanding (Paragraph 6)

5. In your opinion, who is more closed-minded: the Town Mouse or the Country Mouse? What makes you believe that?

~~~~~~

~~~~~~

~~~~~~

~~~~~~

Identifying and Defining Words with Suffixes

 Directions:

Circle the word in each sentence that uses a suffix. Then, on the line below, write a short definition for that word based on your understanding of the suffix.

1. I always try to be cheerful in the morning, but it can be tough!

2. I missed my bus because I was just staring off into space, totally mindless.

3. My Aunt Rachel was a great rugby player when she was in college.

4. Some mushrooms are edible, but many of them can make you sick.

5. My brother loves rocking out to music with his headphones on.

FITNESS

Please be aware of your environment and be safe at all times. If you cannot do an exercise, just try your best.

Repeat these **exercises 3 ROUNDS**

1 - Abs: 3 times

2 - Lunges: 2 times to each leg.
Note: Use your body weight or books as weight to do leg lunges.

3 - Plank: 6 sec.

4 - Run: 50m
Note: Run 25 meters to one side and 25 meters back to the starting position.

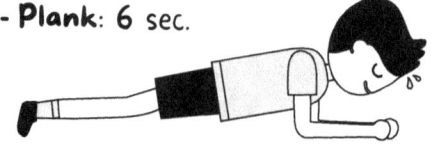

The Whistle
By James Baldwin

Two hundred years ago there lived in Boston a little boy whose name was Benjamin Franklin.

On the day that he was seven years old, his mother gave him a few pennies.

He looked at the bright, yellow pieces and said, "What shall I do with these coppers, mother?"

It was the first money that he had ever had.

"You may buy something, if you wish," said his mother.

"And then will you give me more?" he asked.

His mother shook her head and said: "No, Benjamin. I cannot give you any more. So you must be careful not to spend these foolishly."

The little fellow ran into the street. He heard the pennies jingle in his pocket. How rich he was!

Boston is now a great city, but at that time it was only a little town.

There were not many stores.

As Benjamin ran down the street, he wondered what he should buy. Should he buy candy? He hardly knew how it tasted. Should he buy a pretty toy? If he had been the only child in the family, things might have been different. But there were fourteen boys and girls older than he, and two little sisters who were younger.

What a big family it was! And the father was a poor man. No wonder the lad had never owned a toy.

He had not gone far when he met a larger boy, who was blowing a whistle.

"I wish I had that whistle," he said.

The big boy looked at him and blew it again. Oh, what a pretty sound it made!

"I have some pennies," said Benjamin. He held them in his hand, and showed them to the boy. "You may have them, if you will give me the whistle."

"All of them?"

"Yes, all of them."

"Well, it's a bargain," said the boy; and he gave the whistle to

Benjamin, and took the pennies.

Little Benjamin Franklin was very happy; for he was only seven years old. He ran home as fast as he could, blowing the whistle as he ran.

"See, mother," he said, "I have bought a whistle."

"How much did you pay for it?"

"All the pennies you gave me."

"Oh, Benjamin!"

One of his brothers asked to see the whistle.

"Well, well!" he said. "You've paid a dear price for this thing. It's only a penny whistle, and a poor one at that."

1. What are two specific reasons Benjamin Franklin's mother cannot give him more money in the story?

2. Describe the boy who sells Benjamin the whistle:

3. Which of these words with a suffix describes how Benjamin Franklin was before his mother gave him the pennies?

    A. Wealthiness
    B. Penniless
    C. Whistling
    D. Freedom

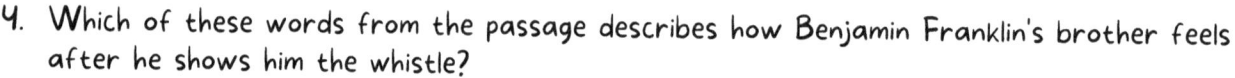

4. Which of these words from the passage describes how Benjamin Franklin's brother feels after he shows him the whistle?

    A. Hugable
    B. Punisher
    C. Regretful
    D. Mocking

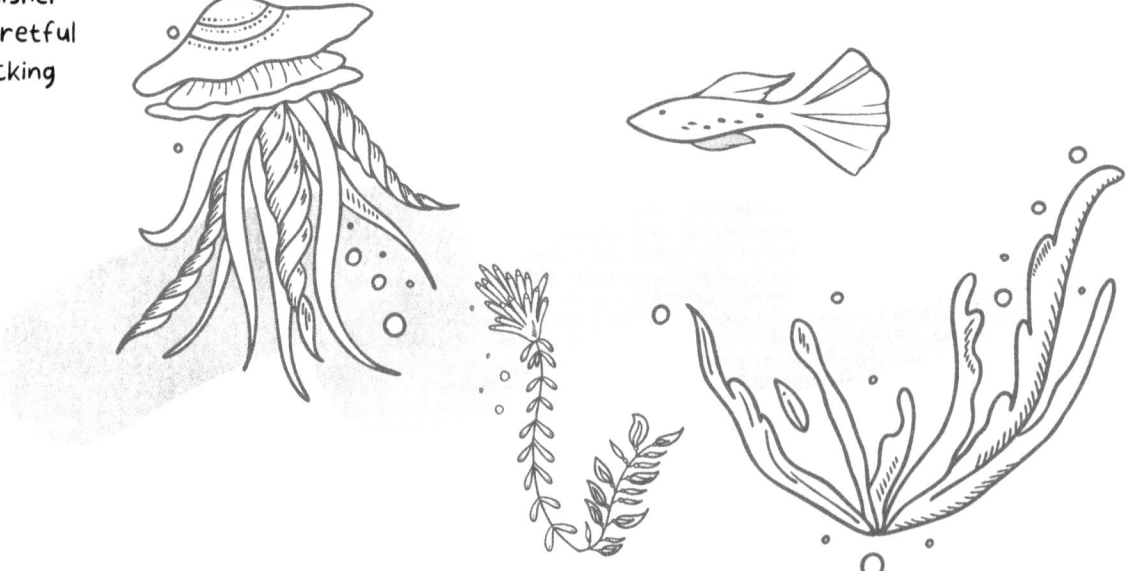

5. Why was it a mistake for Benjamin Franklin to buy that particular whistle?

WEEK 2 DAY 2  ACTIVITIES SUFFIXES

 Directions:

Fill in the blank by adding one of the Common Suffixes to the word in parentheses at the end of the sentence. Be sure to reread the sentence with your new word in place to make sure it makes sense!

1. People with upbeat personalities just seem to be _____ all the time. (JOY)

2. There are several different religious groups in India, but the largest one is _____. (HINDU)

3. After being famous for many years, many celebrities lose interest in their _____. (STAR)

4. Mail carriers always have to double-check to make sure they are delivering letters to the correct person, also called the _____. (ADDRESS)

5. Our soccer team played with a lot of heart this year, but we were _____ because all the other teams in the league were so good. (WIN)

FITNESS

Please be aware of your environment and be safe at all times. If you cannot do an exercise, just try your best.

Repeat these
**exercises
3 ROUNDS**

2 - Side Bending:
5 times to each
side. Note: try to
touch your feet.

1 - Squats: 5 times.
Note: imagine you
are trying to sit on a
chair.

3 - Tree Pose: Stay
as long as possible.
Note: do the same
with the other leg.

WEEK 2 DAY 3  MATH

Diagrams: add/subtract/multiply/divide

1. Which equation does the number line most likely represent?

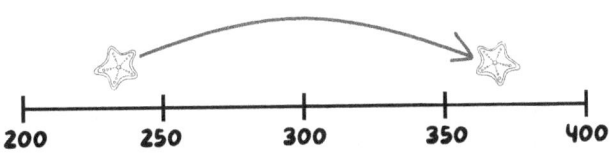

    A. 200 + 350 = 550
    B. 240 + 125 = 365
    C. 250 + 100 = 350
    D. 365 - 240 = 125

2. What is the difference between 48 - 21?

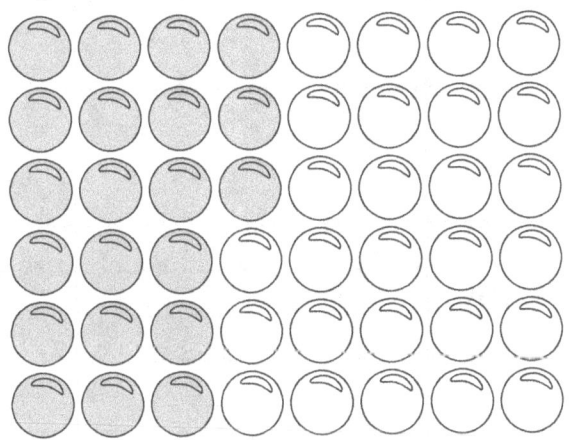

    A. 24
    B. 25
    C. 26
    D. 27

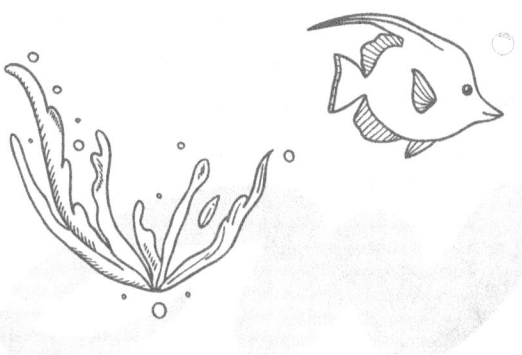

3. What is 7 x 14?

    A. 78
    B. 88
    C. 98
    D. 108

4. Which expression best represents the model below?

    A. 3 + 5
    B. 15 ÷ 5
    C. 15 - 3
    D. 15 - 5

5. Which equation does the number line most likely represent?

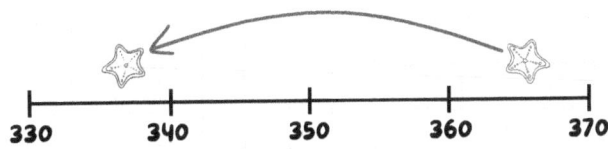

    A. 370 - 335 = 35
    B. 370 - 30 = 40
    C. 365 - 27 = 338
    D. 340 + 27 = 367

6. What is  ?

Each 🐚 has a value of 10.

Answer _____

7. A captain of a spacecraft has **36** buttons on the control panel. Which picture could represent how the buttons are arranged?

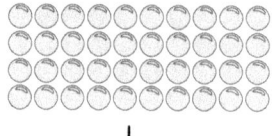

1

2

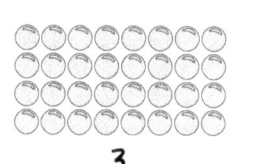

3   4

A. Diagram 1
B. Diagram 2
C. Diagram 3
D. Diagram 4

8. Which expression best represents the action on the number line below?

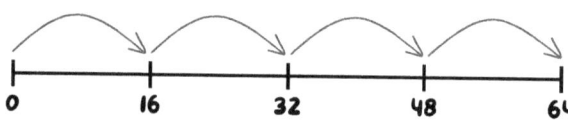

A. 16 x 4
B. 16 + 16 + 16
C. 16 + 4
D. 0 + 16

9. Which expression could represent the picture bellow?

A. 6 x 6 = 36
B. 6 + 7 = 13
C. 42 ÷ 7 = 6
D. 13 - 6 = 7

10. Which situation could be represented by the picture below?

A. 8 classmates each bring 8 pastries to share.

B. 8 classmates each bring 48 pastries to share.

C. 48 pastries are shared equally among 6 classmates.

D. 48 pastries are shared equally among 8 classmates.

FITNESS

Please be aware of your environment and be safe at all times. If you cannot do an exercise, just try your best.

Repeat these **exercises 3 ROUNDS**

1 - Bend forward: 10 times.
Note: try to touch your feet. Make sure to keep your back straight and if needed you can bend your knees.

2 - Lunges: 3 times to each leg.
Note: Use your body weight or books as weight to do leg lunges.

3 - Plank: 6 sec.

4 - Abs: 10 times

WEEK 2 DAY 4  MATH

Diagrams: add/subtract/multiply/divide

1. What is 8 multiplied by 4?

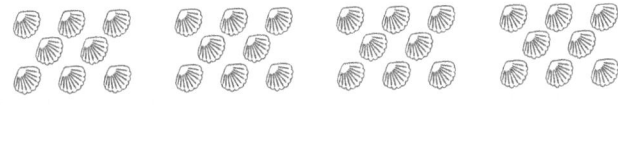

Answer _____

2. Which equation does the number line most likely represent?

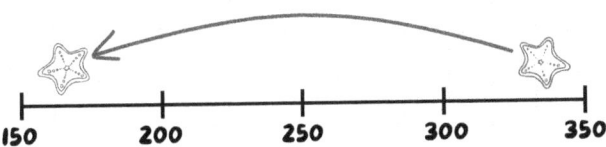

A. 170 + 250 = 420
B. 350 - 200 = 150
C. 330 - 160 = 170
D. 360 - 180 = 180

3. Which expression best represents the action on the number line below?

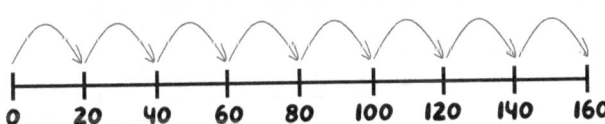

A. 20 + 8
B. 20 x 8
C. 0 + 160
D. 100 + 60

4. What is 240 subtracted from 1,000? Use ⊙ as 10.

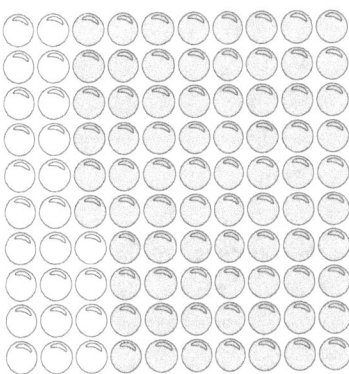

Answer _____

5. Which situation could be represented by the picture below?

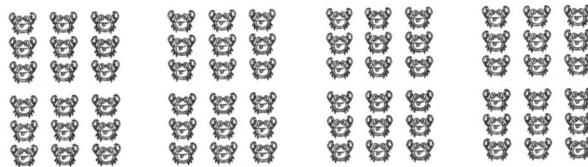

A. 72 crabs are shared equally among 8 men.

B. 9 men each caught and brought 9 crabs to share.

C. 9 men each caught and brought 72 crabs to share.

D. 72 crabs are shared equally among 9 men.

6. Which expression does the number line most likely represent?

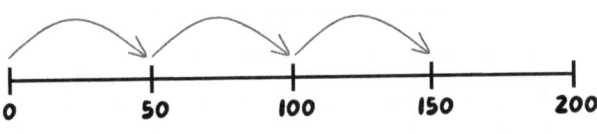

A. 0 + 150
B. 50 x 3
C. 100 + 50
D. 50 x 100

7. What is the value of the diagram below if one 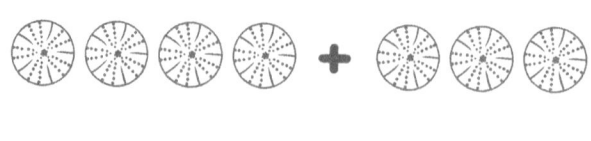 equals 70?

Answer _____

8. Which expression best represents the model below? Use 🐚 as 10.

A. 240 ÷ 4
B. 240 ÷ 40
C. 24 ÷ 60
D. 240 ÷ 6

9. An astronaut has **56** packs of food in the box. Which picture could represent how the packs are arranged?

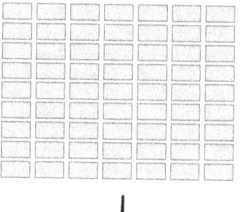

1

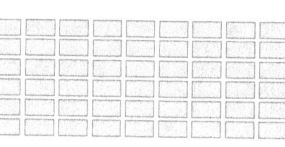

2

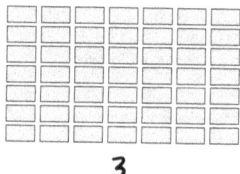

3

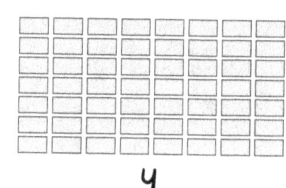

4

A. Diagram 1
B. Diagram 2
C. Diagram 3
D. Diagram 4

10. Which expression could represent the picture bellow? Use 🦔 as 5.

A. 50 + 4
B. 5 x 4
C. 50 x 4
D. 25 x 4

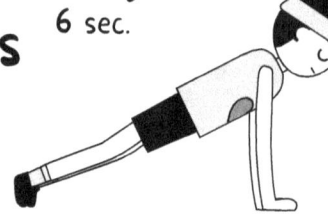

WEEK 2 DAY 5  MATH

Place Value

1. What is the tens place digit in the number 1,038?

   Answer _____

2. In the number 873 the number 8 is in what place value?

   Answer _____

3. How many times less is the digit 3 than the number 300?

   Answer _____

4. The ones place value digit in the number 1,783 is:

   Answer _____

5. In what place value is 2 in the number 2,174?

   A. Ones
   B. Tens
   C. Hundreds
   D. Thousands

6. Which digit represents the hundreds place in the number 1,642?

   A. 1
   B. 2
   C. 4
   D. 6

7. In which of the following numbers is the digit 3 in the greatest place value?

   A. 3,176
   B. 1,639
   C. 2,375
   D. 1,893

8. Ann wrote a number in which the digit 1 is in the greatest place value. Which number did she write?

   A. 2,981
   B. 2,176
   C. 1,234
   D. 3,314

9. The ones place value in the number 4,613 is:

   Answer _____

10. There are 5 ones, 7 hundreds, 2 tens and 3 thousands in the number thought by Jake. What is the number?

    A. 5,372
    B. 3,725
    C. 7,253
    D. 2,537

Standard form vs expanded form

1. Choose the option in which the number 932 is represented in an expanded form.

   A. 90 + 32
   B. 30 + 900 + 2
   C. 300 + 90 + 2
   D. 2 + 32 + 900

2. Which of the following answer choices represents the number one thousand, two hundred and seventy-six in standard form?

   A. 2,762
   B. 6,267
   C. 1,276
   D. 7,621

3. Choose the standard form of the number 5 + 800 + 40.

   A. 8,405
   B. 8,450
   C. 8,045
   D. 845

4. The number 735 in expanded form can be written as:

   A. 700 + 300 + 5
   B. 30 + 700 + 5
   C. 5 + 30 + 70
   D. 730 + 30 + 5

5. Choose the standard form of the number 300 + 8 + 50 + 1,000.

   A. 1,358
   B. 3,158
   C. 8,531
   D. 1,385

6. Write the number three thousand, six hundred and twenty-two in standard form.

   Answer _____

7. Write 8,563 in words.

   Answer _____

   _____

8. What is 50+7,000+4+300 in standard form?

   Answer _____

9. Write the expanded form of the number 2,739 in digits.

   Answer _____

10. What is 8 tens + 4 thousands + 6 ones + 5 hundreds in standard form?

   Answer _____

Please be aware of your environment and be safe at all times. If you cannot do an exercise, just try your best.

1 - **Down Dog**: 10 sec.

2 - **Bend Down**: 10 sec.

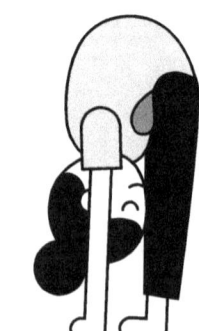

3 - **Chair**: 10 sec.

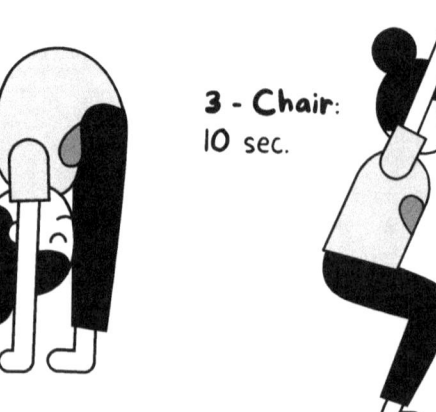

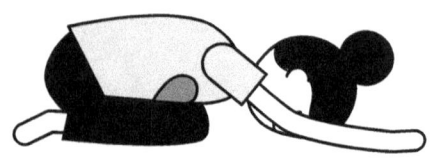

4 - **Child Pose**: 20 sec.

5 - **Shavasana**: as long as you can. Note: think of happy moments and relax your mind.

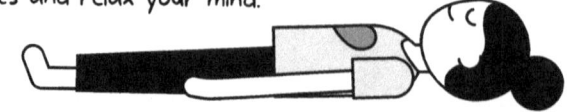

WEEK 2 DAY 6  EXPERIMENT

Racing With Mass

Last week, we introduced the concept of mass and created a balance to help us compare masses. This week, we'll start to look at how the mass of an object affects its ability to move by creating a racetrack! First, we'll build the track, then we'll time our race.

Materials:

- Your balance (See last week's experiment)
- A large, flattened cardboard box
- A ruler or tape measure
- Scissors or a box cutter (be sure to always have an adult help when you use sharp tools!)
- Heavy tape, such as duct tape
- A stop watch or timer
- Several small balls (like golf balls, ping pong balls, marbles, etc.) that fit into the cups on your balance

Procedure:

1. Using your balance, compare the masses of the small balls or spheres you gathered. Using some note paper, rank them from highest mass to lowest mass. Set that information aside.

2. Using the ruler and a black marker, draw three rectangles that are at least 2 feet, 6 inches long and about three inches wide. It's important that all three rectangles are the same size!

3. Ask an adult to help you cut out the three rectangles you just created

4. Using your heavy tape, attach the three rectangles of cardboard to each other so they make a U-shaped trough that looks a little like a rain gutter. This is your racetrack!

5. Prop your completed racetrack against the edge of a sofa, coffee table, or other piece of furniture so that it looks like a ramp with a nice, gradual slope.

6. Gather your timer and the small spheres you compared earlier. One at a time, drop the spheres (don't push or force them!) into the top of the track you've created and measure how long it takes them to reach the floor using the stopwatch. Record this data on the same note paper you used to rank the masses of the objects earlier.

7. Once you've carried out this experiment and answered the follow-up questions below, be sure you save your ramp and your notes, as well as your balance for future experiments!

Follow-Up Questions:

1. What relationship did you notice between the mass of an object and the time it took it to go down the ramp?

2. Was there a certain object you thought would be faster or slower than it wound up being? Which object was it, and why were you surprised?

Please be aware of your environment and be safe at all times. If you cannot do an exercise, just try your best.

3 - Stretching: Stay as long as possible. Note: do on one leg then on another.

1 - Tree Pose: Stay as long as possible. Note: do on one leg then on another.

2 - Down Dog: 10 sec.

6 - Shavasana: 5 min. Note: this pose is very important and provides you with long term benefits. Try not to skip this. Close your eyes and imagine who you want to be and what your goals are! Always think happy thoughts.

5 - Book Pose: 6 sec. Note: Keep your core tight. Legs should be across from your eyes.

4 - Lower Plank: 6 sec. Note: Keep your back straight and body tight.

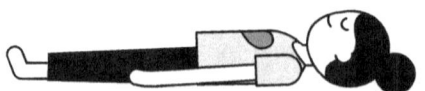

WEEK 2 DAY 7  MAZE

Task: Yikes! All the snakes are tangled up. Go ahead and match the corresponding letters with the numbers.

Rock on!
Practicing math and English concepts is just as important as keeping our body healthy and active. Have you tried our fitness activities?

WEEK 3

Did you know the Blue Whale is the largest animal ever?
Yes, the blue whales are even larger than any known dinosaur!
Blue whales can weigh over **400,000** pounds.

As you read increasingly complex texts, you'll encounter words whose definitions you might not know. Of course, a dictionary or internet search can be used to find a definition quickly, but here are some other strategies you can use to help determine the meanings of words as you read. These strategies can be helpful on tests or other situations when you can't use a dictionary.

Strategy 1: Context Clues
One of the best ways to figure out what a new word means is to study the other words in the sentence and paragraph around it. That extra context provides you with clues.

 For Example...

Sentence: The surgeon took the scalpel from the nurse and made an incision on the patient's chest in order to access his heart.

This sentence has two words that might be unfamiliar: scalpel and incision. However, if we have a good understanding of what's going on in the sentence, the meaning of both words is pretty obvious.

- We know a scalpel is something a surgeon (doctor) uses to access someone's heart.
- We know an incision is what the surgeon makes with the scalpel in order to access the heart.

So, based on those context clues, we can conclude that a scalpel is a knife used by a surgeon, while an incision is a cut made by a scalpel!

Strategy 2: Breaking a Word Down
If you see a big, complex word that you can tell has prefixes and suffixes attached to it, it can be useful to break the word into its parts to help you understand it better.

 For Example...

Sentence: A lot of people assume that living without hot water would be an unmanageable problem, but a shocking number of Americans live that way.

The word unmanageable looks like a monstrous cluster of letters, but let's break it down into a prefix, a root word, and a suffix:

Prefix: Un (not)

Root: manage (to deal with or handle something)

Suffix: able (to do something)

So, when we break the word into three parts, we see that **unmanageable** simply means something that's impossible to handle or deal with!

The Miser
By Aesop

One day, a rich, greedy old man sold all of his possessions, took all his money, and bought a huge gold nugget that represented all of his wealth. Instead of putting it in a vault or showing it off to people, though, the old miser dug a hole on the outskirts of town and buried the gold nugget there. Every day, he would visit the place where the gold was buried, just to be near it.

Eventually, the town where the miser lived began expanding, and a construction crew that was building new houses on what had been the outskirts of town noticed the old man visiting the same spot every day. Eventually they got curious, and when they noticed that the ground had been dug up there at some point in the past, they dug down themselves and discovered the gold nugget, which they sold and split up the money.

The next day, the miser returned to his favorite place and was terrified to discover the empty hole. He began to cry and tear out his hair when one of the construction workers came over to console him.

"Look friend, I'll help you bury a rock in this hole to replace your lost gold. Then, each day, you can come here and know that there's something buried beneath your feet, just like you did before."

"What use will that be?" the old man whined. "A rock is not worth nearly as much as gold!"

"Your gold was of no value anyway," the worker told him, "because you refused to use it."

1. Based on the story, what does the word "Miser" mean?

2. Why does the construction worker say the gold was "of no value anyway?"

3. Which word does the phrase "...the town where the miser lived began expanding..." help the reader understand better?

    A. Outskirts (Paragraph 1)
    B. Construction (Paragraph 2)
    C. Miser (Paragraph 1)
    D. Terrified (Paragraph 3)

4. How did the miser's own behavior directly contribute to his loss?

    A. He invested all of his wealth into one item.
    B. He didn't understand that the gold had no real value because he wouldn't spend it.
    C. The construction workers only got curious about the gold because he kept visiting it.
    D. If he had hidden the gold better, nobody would have found it.

5. Why do you think the miser put all his wealth into one gold nugget and buried it in the first place?

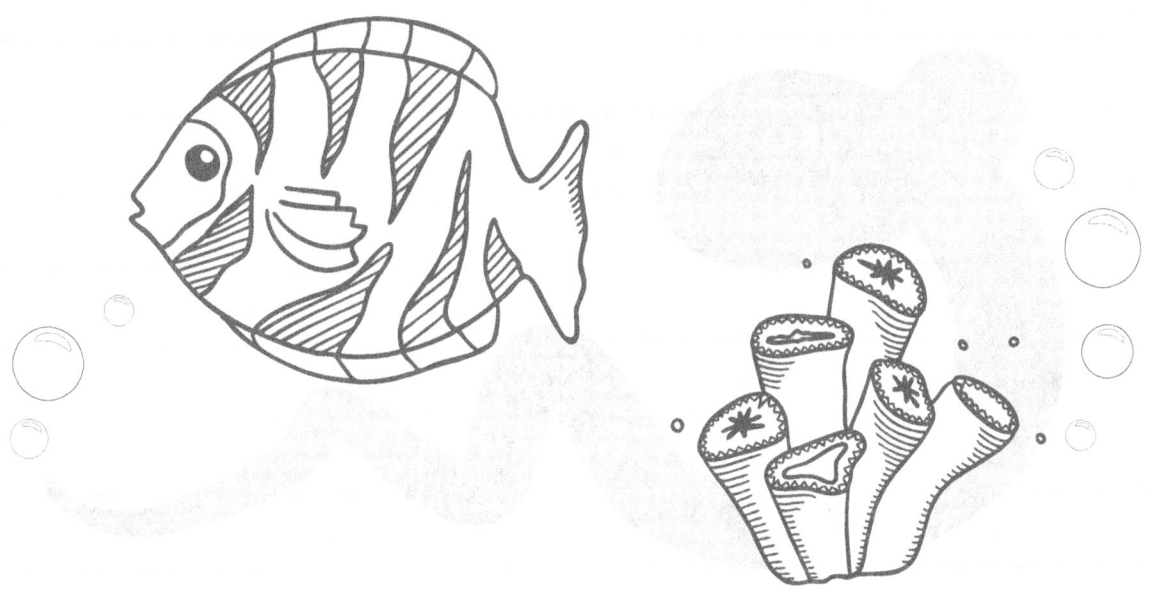

Defining New Words with Context Clues

⭐ **Directions:**

Write a definition for the bold word or words in the sentence on the line below and circle the other words in the sentence that helped you come up with that definition..

1. The magician showed off his skill in **prestidigitation** by doing a variety of card tricks and pulling a rabbit out of a hat.

2. All the teachers and students had to go to the assembly hall for a **convocation** at the beginning of the school year.

3. Mr. Lawrence was awarded a medal for his bravery during the house fire, which is the highest **accolade** he has earned so far.

4. Charlie held back his tears and tried to be **stoic** when he fell, even though his knee was hurting very badly.

5. The students were filled with **ennui** because there was an hour left in the school day, and the teacher had said the only things they could do were read silently or do math problems.

FITNESS

Please be aware of your environment and be safe at all times. If you cannot do an exercise, just try your best.

1 - Abs: 3 times

Repeat these exercises **3 ROUNDS**

2 - Lunges: 2 times to each leg.
Note: Use your body weight or books as weight to do leg lunges.

4 - Run: 50m
Note: Run 25 meters to one side and 25 meters back to the starting position.

3 - Plank: 6 sec.

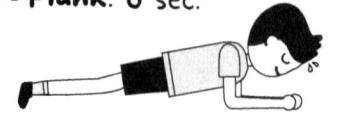

Speaking a Piece
By James Baldwin

Two children, brother and sister, were on their way to school. Both were very small. The boy was only four years old, and the girl was not yet six. "Come, Edward, we must hurry," said the sister. "We must not be late." With one hand the little boy clung to his sister's arm, and with the other he held his primer.

This primer was his only book, and he loved it. It had a bright blue cover, which he was careful not to soil. And in it were some odd little pictures, which he never grew tired of looking at.

Edward could spell nearly all the words in his primer, and he could read quite well.

The school was more than a mile from their home, and the children trotted along as fast as their short legs could carry them.

At a place where two roads crossed, they saw a tall gentleman coming to meet them. He was dressed in black, and had a very pleasant face.

"Oh, Edward, there is Mr. Harris!" whispered the little girl. "Don't forget your manners."

They were glad to see Mr. Harris, for he was the minister. They stopped by the side of the road and made their manners. Edward bowed very gracefully, and his sister curtsied.

"Good morning, children!" said the minister; and he kindly shook hands with both.

"I have something here for little Edward," he said. Then he took from his pocket a sheet of paper on which some verses were written.

"See! It is a little speech that I have written for him. The teacher will soon ask him to speak a piece at school, and I am sure that he can learn this easily and speak it well."

Edward took the paper and thanked the kind minister.

"Mother will help him learn it," said his sister.

"Yes, I will try to learn it," said Edward.

"Do so, my child," said the Minister; "and I hope that when you grow up you will become a wise man and a great orator."

Then the two children hurried on to school.

The speech was not hard to learn, and Edward soon knew every word of it. When the time came for him to speak, his mother and the minister were both there to hear him.

He spoke so well that everybody was pleased. He pronounced every word plainly, as though he were talking to his schoolmates.

1. Write down **four different words** from the story that helped you understand that a "primer" is a kind of book.

2. What details from the passage tell you that, in the world of the text, a "minister" is a highly respected person?

3. Based on the passage, which of these words do you think is the closest in meaning to **"curtsied?"**

    A. Whispered (Paragraph 6)
    B. Stopped (Paragraph 7)
    C. Bowed (Paragraph 7)
    D. Took (Paragraph 9)

4. What detail from earlier in the text predicted that Edward would be good at learning the piece Mr. Harris gave him?

    A. Earlier in the story, it said that Edward was very good at reading, even though he was only four.
    B. Earlier in the story, it said that Mr. Harris was a respected person, so Edward would want to impress him.
    C. Earlier in the story, it said that Edward was the best student in his class.
    D. Earlier in the story, it said that Edward had good manners.

5. Based on the passage, what do you think it means to **"speak a piece?"**

Defining New Words by Breaking Them Down

Directions:

In the space below each sentence, break each word down into its parts: prefix, root word, and suffix. Then, write a definition for the word based on your breakdown

1. Unfortunately, our concert tickets were **nonrefundable**, which meant we couldn't get our money back when it rained.

Prefix: ⁓⁓⁓⁓⁓⁓⁓⁓⁓⁓⁓⁓⁓⁓⁓⁓⁓⁓⁓⁓⁓⁓⁓⁓⁓⁓⁓⁓⁓

Root Word: ⁓⁓⁓⁓⁓⁓⁓⁓⁓⁓⁓⁓⁓⁓⁓⁓⁓⁓⁓⁓⁓⁓⁓⁓

Suffix: ⁓⁓⁓⁓⁓⁓⁓⁓⁓⁓⁓⁓⁓⁓⁓⁓⁓⁓⁓⁓⁓⁓⁓⁓⁓⁓⁓⁓

Definition: ⁓⁓⁓⁓⁓⁓⁓⁓⁓⁓⁓⁓⁓⁓⁓⁓⁓⁓⁓⁓⁓⁓⁓⁓⁓⁓

2. The word "car" is much less impressive than "**automobile**."

Prefix: ⁓⁓⁓⁓⁓⁓⁓⁓⁓⁓⁓⁓⁓⁓⁓⁓⁓⁓⁓⁓⁓⁓⁓⁓⁓⁓⁓⁓

Root Word: ⁓⁓⁓⁓⁓⁓⁓⁓⁓⁓⁓⁓⁓⁓⁓⁓⁓⁓⁓⁓⁓⁓

Definition: ⁓⁓⁓⁓⁓⁓⁓⁓⁓⁓⁓⁓⁓⁓⁓⁓⁓⁓⁓⁓⁓⁓⁓⁓

3. The county judge is an **appointee** of the governor.

Root Word: ⁓⁓⁓⁓⁓⁓⁓⁓⁓⁓⁓⁓⁓⁓⁓⁓⁓⁓⁓⁓⁓⁓

Suffix: ⁓⁓⁓⁓⁓⁓⁓⁓⁓⁓⁓⁓⁓⁓⁓⁓⁓⁓⁓⁓⁓⁓⁓⁓⁓⁓⁓⁓

Definition: ⁓⁓⁓⁓⁓⁓⁓⁓⁓⁓⁓⁓⁓⁓⁓⁓⁓⁓⁓⁓⁓⁓⁓⁓

4. The cornfield was a dry, yellow-brown color and dotted only with **postharvest** stubble from what had been corn stalks.

Prefix: _____

Root Word: _____

Definition: _____

5. My uncle doesn't believe in giving fancy presents or buying the newest technology gadgets because he believes in **anticonsumerism**.

Prefix: _____

Root Word: _____

Suffix: _____

Definition: _____

FITNESS

Please be aware of your environment and be safe at all times. If you cannot do an exercise, just try your best.

Repeat these
**exercises
3 ROUNDS**

3 - Abs:
10 times

4 - High Plank: 6 sec.

1 - Squats: 5 times.
Note: imagine you
are trying to sit on a
chair.

2 - Side Bending:
5 times to each
side. Note: try to
touch your feet.

5 - Tree Pose:
Stay as long as
possible.
Note: do the same
with the other leg.

WEEK 3 DAY 3  MATH

Rounding to nearest 10, 100 and 1,000

1. What is **679** rounded to the nearest hundred?

   A. 670
   B. 680
   C. 600
   D. 700

2. Round **837** to the nearest ten.

   A. 830
   B. 840
   C. 800
   D. 900

3. What is **1,056** rounded to the nearest thousand?

   A. 1,050
   B. 1,100
   C. 1,000
   D. 1,156

4. Which of the following numbers rounded to the nearest hundred gives you **800**?

   A. 784
   B. 853
   C. 745
   D. 739

5. Which of the following numbers rounded to the nearest hundred gives you **1,000**?

   A. 923
   B. 1,562
   C. 976
   D. 943

6. Round **673** to the nearest ten.

   Answer _____

7. Round **2,359** to the nearest thousand.

   Answer _____

8. Which place value do you need to round in the number **4,736** to get **4,700**?

   Answer _____

9. Round **835** and **832** to the nearest ten. Write a number sentence using those two rounded numbers and a comparison symbol.

   Answer _____

10. What is **3,995** rounded to the nearest ten?

    Answer _____

Fraction Comparison Problems

1. Which number sentence below is true?

   A. $\frac{1}{2} = \frac{3}{8}$

   B. $\frac{3}{4} < \frac{3}{5}$

   C. $\frac{2}{3} > \frac{2}{4}$

   D. $\frac{6}{1} < 5$

2. Which expression could represent the picture below?

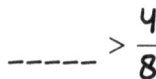

A. $\frac{3}{4} = \frac{2}{4}$

B. $\frac{3}{4} < \frac{2}{4}$

C. $\frac{3}{4} > \frac{2}{4}$

D. $\frac{3}{4} = \frac{1}{4}$

3. Which fraction can be used to make the number sentence true?

$$\text{-----} > \frac{4}{8}$$

A. $\frac{5}{6}$

B. $\frac{3}{9}$

C. $\frac{2}{5}$

D. $\frac{3}{7}$

4. Ian drank $\frac{2}{4}$ of his orange juice and Becky drank $\frac{1}{2}$ of hers. Which statement is true?

A. $\frac{2}{4} > \frac{1}{2}$

B. $\frac{2}{4} < \frac{1}{2}$

C. $\frac{2}{4} = \frac{1}{2}$

D. $\frac{2}{4} \neq \frac{1}{2}$

5. Find the fraction that makes the number sentence true.

$$\frac{4}{8} < \text{----}$$

A. $\frac{3}{8}$

B. $\frac{3}{4}$

C. $\frac{1}{2}$

D. $\frac{1}{4}$

FITNESS

Repeat these **exercises 3 ROUNDS**

Please be aware of your environment and be safe at all times. If you cannot do an exercise, just try your best.

1 - Bend forward: 10 times.
Note: try to touch your feet. Make sure to keep your back straight and if needed you can bend your knees.

2 - Lunges: 3 times to each leg.
Note: Use your body weight or books as weight to do leg lunges.

3 - Plank: 6 sec.

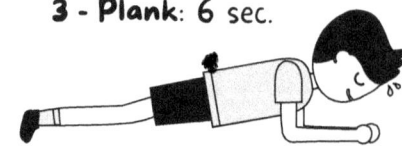

4 - Abs: 10 times

WEEK 3 DAY 4  MATH

Fraction Comparison Problems

1. Compare $\frac{1}{3}$ and $\frac{2}{4}$ using a comparison symbol.

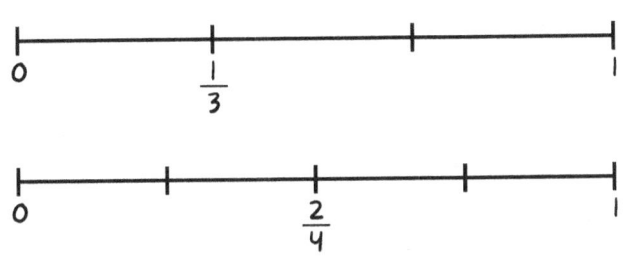

Answer _____

2. Put $\frac{4}{10}$, $\frac{1}{2}$, $\frac{3}{5}$ on the number line.

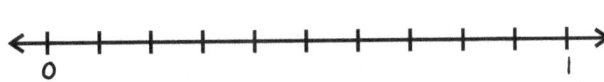

3. Complete the equation $7 = \frac{7}{?}$

Answer _____

4. A captain eats $\frac{1}{2}$ plate of rice and $\frac{2}{3}$ cup of tea. Which statement is true?

A. $\frac{1}{2} > \frac{2}{3}$

B. $\frac{1}{2} < \frac{2}{3}$

C. $\frac{1}{2} = \frac{2}{3}$

D. $\frac{2}{3} < \frac{1}{2}$

5. Compare $\frac{5}{6}$ and $\frac{2}{3}$ using a comparison symbol.

Answer _____

Fractions with diagrams

1. What fraction is represented by the model below?

A. $\frac{3}{4}$

B. $\frac{8}{3}$

C. $\frac{3}{8}$

D. $\frac{4}{3}$

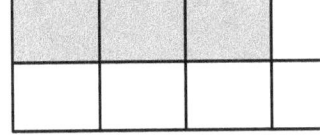

2. Which fraction shows the shaded portion for the model below?

A. $\frac{1}{4}$ or one half

B. $\frac{4}{16}$ or one half

C. $\frac{1}{16}$ or one fourth

D. $\frac{4}{16}$ or one fourth

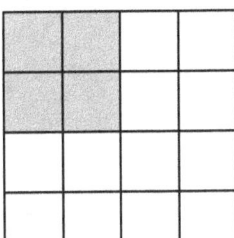

3. Which of the following pictures represents four-sixths?

A.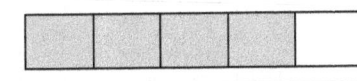

B.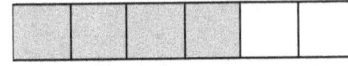

C.

D.

59

4. What is the fraction that represents the UNSHADED portion in the model below?

A. $\dfrac{2}{9}$

B. $\dfrac{7}{2}$

C. $\dfrac{7}{9}$

D. $\dfrac{2}{7}$

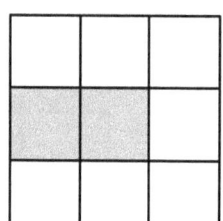

5. Using the model below, which number sentence is FALSE?

A. $\dfrac{12}{36} = \dfrac{3}{9}$

B. $\dfrac{12}{36} = \dfrac{1}{3}$

C. $\dfrac{3}{9} = \dfrac{1}{3}$

D. $\dfrac{6}{36} = \dfrac{3}{9}$

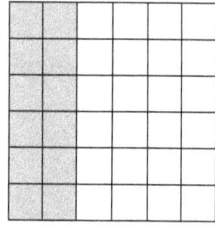

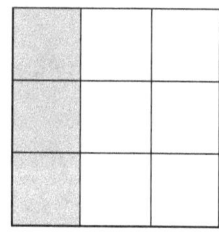

6. Write a statement represented by the model below.

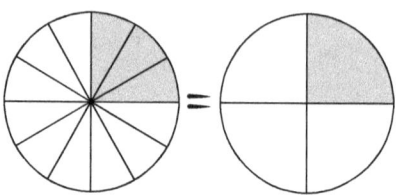

Answer _____

7. Write in the missing fraction for the number line below.

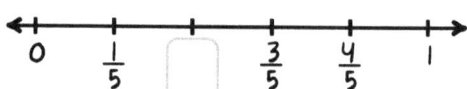

Answer _____

8. Write a fraction to represent the shaded portion for the model below.

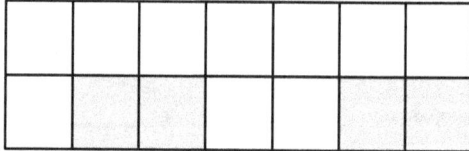

Answer _____

FITNESS

Please be aware of your environment and be safe at all times. If you cannot do an exercise, just try your best.

Repeat these **exercises 3 ROUNDS**

1 - High Plank: 6 sec.

2 - Chair: 10 sec. Note: sit on an imaginary chair, keep your back straight.

3 - Waist Hooping: 10 times. Note: if you do not have a hoop, pretend you have an imaginary hoop and rotate your hips 10 times.

4 - Abs: 10 times

WEEK 3 DAY 5  MATH

Fractions with diagrams

1. Which fractions are missing from the number line below?

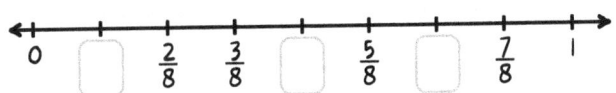

Answer _____

2. Complete the statement represented by the model below.

$$\frac{?}{15} = \frac{2}{?}$$

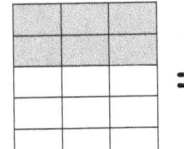 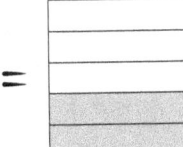

Answer _____

Fractions: add/subtract and multiply (Same denominator)

1. Using the model below, which number sentence is true?

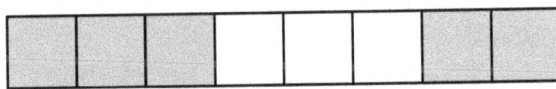

A. $\frac{1}{8} + \frac{1}{8} + \frac{1}{8} = \frac{2}{8}$

B. $\frac{1}{8} + \frac{1}{8} + \frac{1}{8} = \frac{3}{8}$

C. $\frac{3}{8} + \frac{2}{8} = \frac{5}{8}$

D. $\frac{3}{8} + \frac{3}{8} = \frac{2}{8}$

2. What is the sum of $\frac{2}{6}$ and $\frac{3}{6}$?

A. $\frac{5}{12}$

B. $\frac{5}{6}$

C. $\frac{23}{66}$

D. $\frac{6}{36}$

3. Use the model below to find $\frac{2}{9} \times 3$.

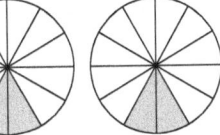

A. $\frac{6}{9}$

B. $\frac{6}{27}$

C. $\frac{6}{18}$

D. $\frac{3}{9}$

4. What is $\frac{5}{6} - \frac{3}{6}$?

A. $\frac{3}{6}$

B. $\frac{1}{6}$

C. $\frac{2}{6}$

D. $\frac{4}{6}$

5. What is $\frac{5}{14}$ subtracted from $\frac{12}{14}$?

A. $\frac{2}{14}$

B. $\frac{6}{14}$

C. $\frac{5}{14}$

D. $\frac{7}{14}$

6. Which number sentence is modeled below?

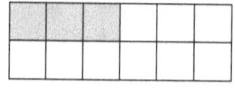 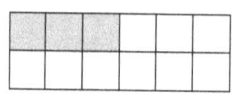
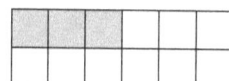 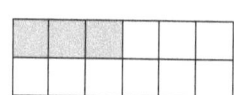

A. $\frac{1}{12} \times 4 = \frac{4}{12}$

B. $\frac{3}{12} \times 4 = \frac{12}{12}$

C. $\frac{3}{6} \times 4 = \frac{12}{6}$

D. $\frac{4}{12} \times 3 = \frac{12}{12}$

7. Write a subtraction statement represented by the model below.

$$\frac{6}{10} - \frac{?}{10} = \frac{2}{10}$$

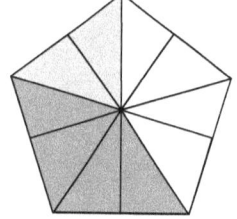

Answer _____

8. What is another way to write $\frac{1}{8} + \frac{1}{8} + \frac{1}{8} + \frac{1}{8} + \frac{1}{8}$?

Answer _____

9. Find $3 \times \frac{2}{7}$.

Answer _____

10. What is $\frac{3}{9}$ added to $\frac{1}{9}$ and then multiplied by 2?

Answer _____

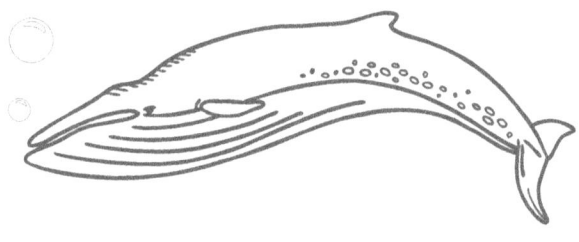

YOGA

Please be aware of your environment and be safe at all times. If you cannot do an exercise, just try your best.

1 - Down Dog: 10 sec.

2 - Bend Down: 10 sec.

3 - Chair: 10 sec.

5 - Shavasana: as long as you can. Note: think of happy moments and relax your mind.

4 - Child Pose: 20 sec.

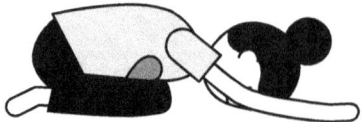

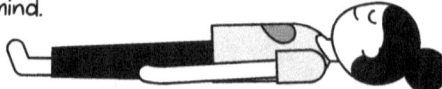

WEEK 3 DAY 6 🐋 EXPERIMENT

How Force Affects Motion

This week, we'll be using our balance and racetrack to continue building an understanding of how mass, motion, and force are related. Force is a push or pull that affects an object's motion.

Materials:

🐟   Your balance (See last Week 1's experiment)

🐟   Your racetrack (See Week 2's experiment)

🐟   A ruler or tape measure

🐟   A stopwatch or timer

🐟   Several small balls (like golf balls, ping pong balls, marbles, etc.) that fit into the cups on your balance

🐟   Your notes from Week 2's experiment

Procedure:

1. Using your balance, compare the masses of the small balls or spheres you gathered. Using some note paper, rank them from highest mass to lowest mass. Set that information aside. (NOTE: If you're using the same objects you did last week and you still have your notes, you can skip this step and just review what you already have written down.)

2. Set up your racetrack like you did last week and practice placing balls at the top of the ramp and giving them a push. Last week, we were just dropping objects into the ramp, but this time, we want to put a little force behind them. Your goal is to make the amount of force you're giving with each push the same. Practice giving the objects a "little push" and a "big push."

3. Gather your timer and the small spheres you compared earlier, and one at a time, place the spheres into the top of the track you've created and give them a little push down the ramp. Using the stopwatch, measure how long it takes them to reach the floor. Record this data on the same note paper you used to rank the masses of the objects earlier (and, ideally, the times you recorded last week).

4. After you've recorded all your "little push" times, it's time for the big push! Place each object at the top of the ramp, give it a big push down, and record the time.

5. After you've done two runs for all your spheres (a little push run and a big push run), take a look at your notes and answer the questions below.

6. Be sure to save your balance, your racetrack, and your notes for next week's experiment!

WEEK 3 DAY 6  EXPERIMENT

Follow-Up Questions:

1. How do the times for the pushed objects compare to the times for the dropped objects (last week)?

2. How did the mass of the object seem to change the way your pushes affected the time?

Please be aware of your environment and be safe at all times. If you cannot do an exercise, just try your best.

1 - Tree Pose: Stay as long as possible. Note: do on one leg then on another.

2 - Down Dog: 10 sec.

3 - Stretching: Stay as long as possible. Note: do on one leg then on another.

4 - Lower Plank: 6 sec. Note: Keep your back straight and body tight.

5 - Book Pose: 6 sec. Note: Keep your core tight. Legs should be across from your eyes.

6 - Shavasana: 5 min. Note: this pose is very important and provides you with long term benefits. Try not to skip this. Close your eyes and imagine who you want to be and what your goals are! Always think happy thoughts.

WEEK 3 DAY 7 🐋 MAZE

Task: Looks like the cassete tapes have been tangled up. Find the cassete tape that is connected to the cassete player.

Keep at it!

This week we will learn about commonly confused words, talk about fractions, and learn about friction.

WEEK 4

It's a seahorse!

Did you know seahorses do not have teeth or a stomach? Since seahorses do not have a stomach, they must eat often to stay alive.

Written English can be complex because there are a lot of words that sound the same when we speak, but they actually have totally different meanings on the page. When two words with different meanings sound the same, we call them homonyms. If two homonyms are spelled differently in writing, we call those homophones.

When we write, it's really important to pay attention to words that have homophones so we can be sure to choose the right spelling.

 Key Terms

Homonyms: Words that sound the same when spoken

Homophones: Words that sound the same when spoken, but have different definitions and different spellings

NOTE: All homophones are homonyms. **Not** all homonyms are homophones!

For Example...

Sentence 1: My aunt and uncle are very proud of their new car.
Sentence 2: I think I left the ball over there, by the fence.

Their and there are homophones. They sound the same when you read the sentence out loud, but they have different spellings and unique meanings.

Sentence 1: Mrs. Fletcher bought two tickets to the baseball game.
Sentence 2: After I saw my sister with ice cream, I wanted dessert, too!

Two and too are homophones. They sound the same when you read the sentence out loud, but they have different spellings and unique meanings.

Common Homophones:

Prefix	Definition	Example
There	A word that refers to a place, location, or direction	Look over there!
Their	A possessive pronoun that shows ownership	Sally and Steve are very proud of their house.
They're	A contraction (shortened form) of "They are"	I don't like hanging out with my cousins because they're always getting into trouble.
To	A word that usually refers to a direction something is moving or being given	1. I walked to school this morning. 2. I gave a toaster to Mom for her birthday.
Two	The number between one and three (2)	A bicycle has two wheels.
Too	Also or as well	I want cheesecake, too!
Hole	An opening or hollow place	My dog keeps digging holes in the back yard.
Whole	All of something; the entirety of something	The whole class had lunch detention because nobody would admit to throwing the paper airplane.
It's	A contraction (shortened form) of "It is"	It's a beautiful day outside!
Its	A possessive pronoun that shows ownership	The squirrel waved its bushy tail in the air.

The Fox and the Woodcutter
By Aesop

One day, a fox was minding its own business in the woods when a pack of hounds belonging to some hunters discovered it and began to give chase. The fox had heard the clumsy hounds coming from a mile away and gotten a head start, but it knew that if it couldn't find shelter, the hounds would eventually catch up to him or, worse yet, the hunters might appear.

The fox ran into a woodcutter, who was chopping down a tree for firewood. The fox begged the woodsman for help, promising him that he'd find a way to repay the favor somehow. The woodcutter agreed to protect the fox and brought him back to his hut, where he hid him in a corner behind some boxes and blankets.

Eventually, the hounds led the hunters to the woodcutter's house, and the hunters knocked on the door to ask if he had seen a fox.

"No, I haven't seen any fox," the woodcutter said, although he pointed to the corner where the fox was hiding as he said it. "No foxes have come through here at all. There definitely aren't any foxes in my hut right now," he repeated, pointing violently toward the spot where there was a fox in the hut.

Now, the fox was peering out through a small gap in the blankets that covered it in the corner, so it knew that the woodcutter had betrayed its trust. However, the hunters were too eager to catch the fox and failed to pick up on the woodsman's pointing. Instead, they took him at his word and left, continuing deeper into the woods to find the fox.

As soon as they were gone, the fox jumped out of the corner and ran for the door.

"Come back here, you ungrateful fox!" the woodcutter cried out. "You promised to repay me!"

"Repay you?" the fox called back. "I would have gladly repaid you if your actions were as good as your words," it said, bounding away to find another safe place.

1. What is the major conflict or problem the fox is dealing with in this story?

2. What would you say is the "moral" or "message" of this story? Why do you say that?

3. Which of these sentences correctly uses the word "its," as it is used in the sentence, "...so it knew that the woodcutter had betrayed its trust..."?

   A. Its a beautiful day outside!
   B. I can't eat ice cream because its too cold for my teeth.
   C. The fox wagged its tail with joy.
   D. I don't like to play outside when its too hot.

4. Which of these sentences correctly uses the word "there," as it is used in the sentence, "There definitely aren't any foxes in my hut right now?"

   A. My grandparents got a flat tire on there car.
   B. I don't like cats because there too private.
   C. Meet me there after school so we can study together.
   D. Teddy and Maria are hoping to improve there grades.

5. In your opinion, which character's actions in the story are the worst: the fox, the hunters, or the woodsman? Explain your choice.

Identifying Homophone Usage Errors

✦ **Directions:**

Each sentence below contains a bold word which has potential homophones. On the line below the sentence, write whether the word is the Correct or Incorrect form. If the usage is wrong, write the correct form of the word on the line as well.

1. I love camping with my dad's family because **their** all very passionate about the outdoors.

2. I swear my printer has a life of **it's** own: every time I change the paper, it just jams!

3. For **our** vacation, my family and I are traveling to Houston, Texas.

4. I ate a **hole** apple, including the stem and seeds, which made me feel sick.

5. I started the day off with **too** pencils, but now I can't find either one of them.

FITNESS

Please be aware of your environment and be safe at all times. If you cannot do an exercise, just try your best.

Repeat these **exercises 3 ROUNDS**

1 - Abs: 3 times

2 - Lunges: 2 times to each leg.
Note: Use your body weight or books as weight to do leg lunges.

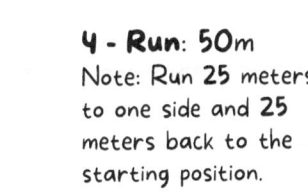

3 - Plank: 6 sec.

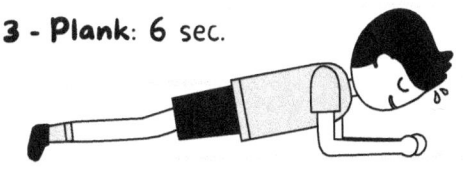

4 - Run: 50m
Note: Run **25** meters to one side and **25** meters back to the starting position.

The Ettrick Shepherd
By James Baldwin

In Scotland there once lived a poor shepherd whose name was James Hogg. His father and grand-father and great-grandfather had all been shepherds.

It was his business to take care of the sheep which belonged to a rich landholder by the Ettrick Water. Sometimes he had several hundreds of lambs to look after. He drove these to the pastures on the hills and watched them day after day while they fed on the short green grass.

He had a dog which he called Sirrah. This dog helped him watch the sheep. He would drive them from place to place as his master wished. Sometimes he would take care of the whole flock while the shepherd was resting or eating his dinner.

One dark night James Hogg was on the hilltop with a flock of seven hundred lambs. Sirrah was with him. Suddenly a storm came up. There was thunder and lightning; the wind blew hard; the rain poured.

The poor lambs were frightened. The shepherd and his dog could not keep them together. Some of them ran towards the east, some towards the west, and some towards the south.

The shepherd soon lost sight of them in the darkness. With his lighted lantern in his hand, he went up and down the rough hills calling for his lambs.

Two or three other shepherds joined him in the search. All night long they sought for the lambs.

Morning came and still they sought. They looked, as they thought, in every place where the lambs might have taken shelter.

At last James Hogg said, "It's of no use; all we can do is to go home and tell the master that we have lost his whole flock."

They had walked a mile or two towards home, when they came to the edge of a narrow and deep ravine. They looked down, and at the bottom they saw some lambs huddled together among the rocks. And there was Sirrah standing guard over them and looking all around for help "These must be the lambs that rushed off towards the south," said James Hogg.

The men hurried down and soon saw that the flock was a large one.

"I really believe they are all here," said one.

They counted them and were surprised to find that not one lamb of the great flock of seven hundred was missing.

How had Sirrah managed to get the three scattered divisions together? How had he managed to drive all the frightened little animals into this place of safety?

Nobody could answer these questions. But there was no shepherd in

Scotland that could have done better than Sirrah did that night.

1. Based on the passage, how would you describe James Hogg?

~~~~~~

~~~~~~

2. Why does the narrator say, "There was no shepherd in Scotland that could have done better than Sirrah did that night?"

~~~~~~

~~~~~~

~~~~~~

3. Which of these sentences correctly uses the word "to," as it is used in the sentence, "...the sheep which belonged to a rich landholder."

   A. Cherry is my favorite flavor for popsicles, but I like watermelon to.
   B. I gave a big, red card to my mother on Valentine's Day.
   C. We only brought to bottles of water on an eight-mile hike.
   D. I wanted to go swimming on our vacation, but it was to rainy.

4. Which of these sentences correctly uses the word "there," as it is used in the sentence, "There was no shepherd in Scotland that could have done better than Sirrah..."

   A. Even though there annoying sometimes, I love my little cousins very much.
   B. When football players crash into each other, there heads can get injured badly.
   C. I think that there just jealous of us!
   D. We were delayed because there was a flock of turkeys blocking the road.

5. In your opinion, who is a more important character in this story: James Hogg or Sirrah the dog? What makes you say that?

~~~~~~

~~~~~~

~~~~~~

WEEK 4 DAY 2  ACTIVITIES
COMMONLY CONFUSED WORDS

 Directions:

Fill in the blank by adding the correct word from the set of homophones in parentheses at the end of the sentence. Be sure to double-check the sentence with your new word in place to make sure it makes sense!

1. The sand at that beach is very rocky, so wear sandals when you walk _____. (THERE / THEIR / THEY'RE)

2. Suddenly, a _____ opened up in the middle of the intersection, causing cars to slam on their brakes. (WHOLE / HOLE)

3. In 1803, the French government sold over **800,000** square miles of land _____ the United States in what is now called "The Louisiana Purchase." (TWO / TO / TOO)

4. The wheelbarrow was useless because the wheel had broken off of _____ axel. (ITS / IT'S)

5. California is famous for _____ beautiful scenery and rich history. (ITS / IT'S)

Please be aware of your environment and be safe at all times. If you cannot do an exercise, just try your best.

Repeat these
exercises
3 ROUNDS

2 - Side Bending:
5 times to each side. Note: try to touch your feet.

1 - Squats: 5 times.
Note: imagine you are trying to sit on a chair.

3 - Tree Pose: Stay as long as possible. Note: do the same with the other leg.

WEEK 4 DAY 3  MATH

Shading in fraction models

1. Which fraction of the shape is shaded?

   A. $\frac{3}{10}$

   B. $\frac{3}{15}$

   C. $\frac{1}{3}$

   D. $\frac{12}{15}$

2. How can we calculate the shaded area?

   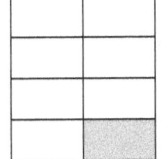 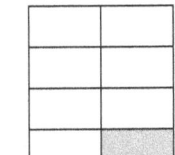 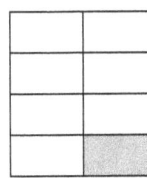

   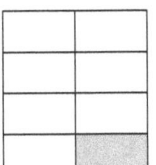 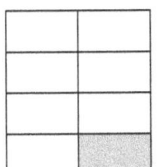 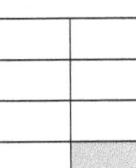

   Answer _____

3. What is $\frac{1}{5}$ subtracted from $\frac{4}{5}$?

   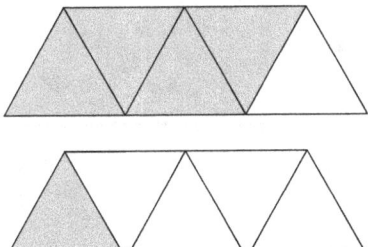

   Answer _____

4. What fraction represents the shaded portion on the model below?

   A. $\frac{3}{9}$

   B. $\frac{6}{3}$

   C. $\frac{3}{6}$

   D. $\frac{6}{9}$

   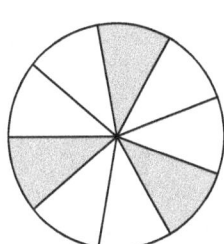

5. Write a fraction for the shaded portion for the model below.

   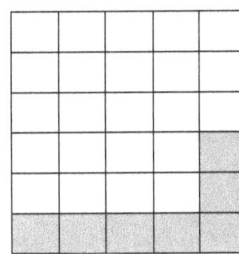

   Answer _____

Comparing numbers using comparison symbols (<, >, =)

1. Which of the following number sentences is true?

   A. 579 < 581
   B. 1,762 > 1,801
   C. 349 = 359
   D. 2,681 < 1,986

2. Compare 984 and 976 using a comparison symbol.

   Answer _____

3. Which expression is true?

    A. 683 > 689
    B. 1,274 < 1,269
    C. 579 < 591
    D. 819 > 831

4. Compare 564 - 176 and 348 using a comparison symbol.

    Answer _____

5. Which symbol would make this inequality true?

    1,187 _____ 1,179

    A. >
    B. <
    C. =
    D. +

6. Which number sentence is true?

    A. 534 = 175 + 349
    B. 863 > 574 + 279
    C. 635 < 268 + 357
    D. 437 = 232 + 215

7. Compare the numbers 869 and 894 using a comparison symbol.

    Answer _____

8. What is the missing number?

    1,358 < _____

    A. 1,349
    B. 1,352
    C. 1,361
    D. 1,344

9. Compare the numbers 1,329 and 1,316 using a comparison symbol.

    Answer _____

10. Compare 456 + 138 and 256 + 338 using a comparison symbol.

    Answer _____

Repeat these **exercises 3 ROUNDS**

Please be aware of your environment and be safe at all times. If you cannot do an exercise, just try your best.

1 - Bend forward: 10 times.
Note: try to touch your feet. Make sure to keep your back straight and if needed you can bend your knees.

2 - Lunges: 3 times to each leg.
Note: Use your body weight or books as weight to do leg lunges.

3 - Plank: 6 sec.

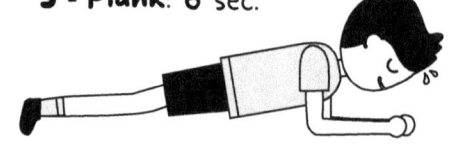

4 - Abs:
10 times

WEEK 4 DAY 4  MATH

Area and perimeter

1. Find the perimeter of the shape below.

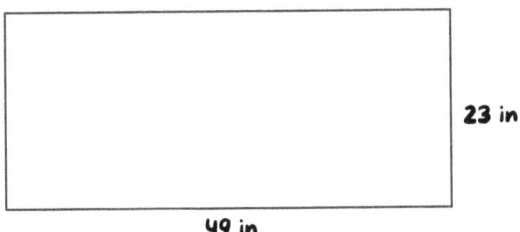

49 in
23 in

A. 134 in
B. 144 in
C. 154 in
D. 164 in

2. Find the perimeter of the shape below.

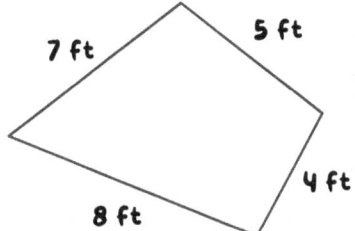

7 ft
5 ft
8 ft
4 ft

A. 24 ft
B. 25 ft
C. 28 ft
D. 29 ft

3. The perimeter of a square is **68** yards. What is the length of one of the sides?

Answer _____

4. A rectangle measures **8** inches in width. The length is **3** times as long as its width. Find the perimeter of the rectangle.

Answer _____

5. The perimeter of this quadrilateral is **72** yards. What is the value of k?

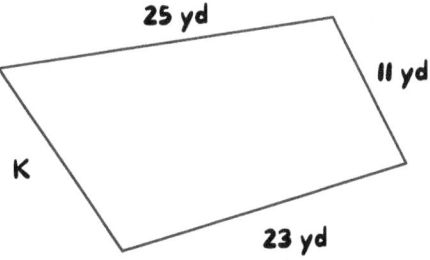

25 yd
11 yd
K
23 yd

Answer _____

6. What is the area of this rectangle?

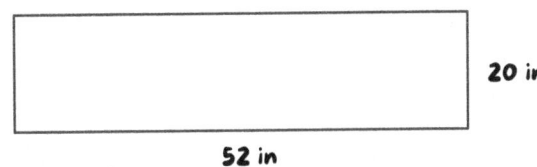

20 in
52 in

A. 1,020 sq in
B. 1,030 sq in
C. 1,040 sq in
D. 1,050 sq in

7. One side of a square is **8** feet long. What is its area?

A. 56 sq ft
B. 64 sq ft
C. 72 sq ft
D. 81 sq ft

8. What is the area of the shape below?

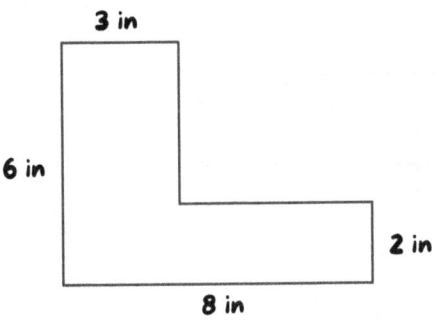

3 in
6 in
2 in
8 in

A. 24 sq in
B. 32 sq in
C. 22 sq in
D. 28 sq in

9. The model below represent sections that are covered with trees. The area of the entire model is 18 square yards. What is the total area of the trees (shaded portion) in square yards?

A. 12 sq yd
B. 4 sq yd
C. 6 sq yd
D. 2 sq yd

10. The area of a rectangle is 63 sq cm. The length is 9 cm. What is the width of the rectangle?

A. 6 cm
B. 7 cm
C. 8 cm
D. 9 cm

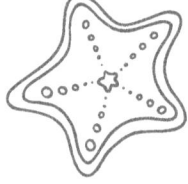

Identifying number patterns

1. The rule for the pattern shown below is "+ 3". Fill in the missing numbers.
3, 6, ..., 12, ..., 18

Answer _____

2. Tammy listed these numbers: 2, 6, 18, 54, 162. What rule did Tammy use?

A. Add 2
B. Add 3
C. Times 2
D. Times 3

3. The chart below shows how many comics James drew.

Monday	Tuesday	Wednesday
2	8	14

Thursday	Friday	Saturday
20	26	32

If the pattern continues, how many comics will James draw on Sunday?

A. 34 comics
B. 36 comics
C. 38 comics
D. 39 comics

Please be aware of your environment and be safe at all times. If you cannot do an exercise, just try your best.

FITNESS

Repeat these exercises **3 ROUNDS**

1 - High Plank: 6 sec.

3 - Waist Hooping: 10 times.
Note: if you do not have a hoop, pretend you have an imaginary hoop and rotate your hips 10 times.

2 - Chair: 10 sec.
Note: sit on an imaginary chair, keep your back straight.

4 - Abs: 10 times

WEEK 4 DAY 5  MATH

Identifying number patterns

1. Look at the pattern below.

   A. What "rule" is being used?

   Answer _____

   B. What might the next shape look like?

   Answer _____

2. Willy recorded the hours he practiced math each week before the test. If this pattern continues, how many hours will he practice on Week 7?

Week 1	Week 2	Week 3
5	9	13

Week 4	Week 5
17	21

   A. 25 hours
   B. 27 hours
   C. 29 hours
   D. 31 hours

3. The number pattern is "times 7". Which number is after 1, 7, 49?

   A. 249
   B. 343
   C. 379
   D. 423

4. The rule for the pattern shown is "+ 12". Fill in the missing numbers.
   10, ..., 34, 46, ..., 70

   Answer _____

5. Which rule describes the pattern: 4, 19, 34, 49?

   Answer _____

6. If the rule is "times 2", which of these numbers could be in the pattern 3, 6, 12, ...?

   A. 88
   B. 86
   C. 94
   D. 96

7. The rule for the pattern shown below is "add 5". Fill in the missing numbers.
   12, ..., ..., 27, ..., 37.

   Answer _____

Tables/Charts and understanding data

Using the following chart, answer questions 1 - 2. The family went on a picnic and brought some sandwiches, apples and cartons of juice. They made a table of the food they brought:

Food			
How many?	16	12	8

1. How many sandwiches did they bring?

   Answer _____

2. How many more apples than cartons of juice did they bring?

   A. 4
   B. 5
   C. 6
   D. 8

Use the following pictograph to answer questions 3 - 4.

Favorite Animals on our Street

Kellie went to local store and bought some oranges, cucumbers, eggs, and chocolate bars. Using the following chart, answer questions 5 - 6.

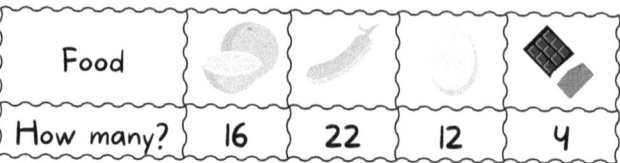

Food	🍊	🥒	🥚	🍫
How many?	16	22	12	4

3. Which animal is the most popular on our Street?

   A. Cat
   B. Dog
   C. Rabbit
   D. They are all equal

4. How many more cats are favored than rabbits?

   Answer _____

5. Which item did Kellie buy the most?

   A. Oranges
   B. Cucumbers
   C. Eggs
   D. Chocolate bars

6. How many more oranges than eggs did she buy?

   A. 10
   B. 6
   C. 4
   D. 12

YOGA

Please be aware of your environment and be safe at all times. If you cannot do an exercise, just try your best.

1 - Down Dog: 10 sec.

2 - Bend Down: 10 sec.

3 - Chair: 10 sec.

4 - Child Pose: 20 sec.

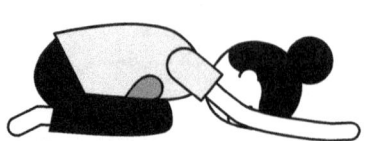

5 - Shavasana: as long as you can. Note: think of happy moments and relax your mind.

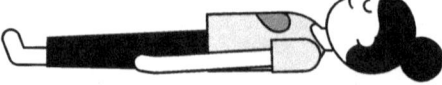

WEEK 4 DAY 6 ⬤ EXPERIMENT

How Friction Affects Motion

This week, we'll be using our balance and racetrack to continue building an understanding of how mass, motion, force, and friction are related. Friction is the resistance you feel when you try to push a heavy object along the floor. Like mass and force, friction has a major impact on motion!

Materials:

- Your balance (See Week 1's experiment)
- Your racetrack (See Week 2's experiment)
- A stopwatch or timer
- Several small balls (like golf balls, ping pong balls, marbles, etc.) that fit into the cups on your balance
- Your notes from Week 2 and Week 3's experiments
- A few pieces of rough sandpaper
- A few cotton balls
- Tape
- Scissors

Procedure:

1. Using your balance, compare the masses of the small balls or spheres you gathered. Using some note paper, rank them from highest mass to lowest mass. Set that information aside. (NOTE: If you're using the same objects you did last week and you still have your notes, you can skip this step and just review what you already have written down.)

2. Cut a few pieces of sandpaper that are the same width as the bottom of your track. Then, using the tape, place a few sections of sandpaper along the track. This will create some friction!

3. Take a few cotton balls and gently pull them apart so they create a spiderweb-like pad. Using the tape, attach a few fuzzy pieces of cotton ball along the track. This will create some more friction!

4. Set up your track so it's ready for racing. Gather your timer and the small spheres you compared earlier. One at a time, drop the spheres (don't push or force them!) into the top of the track you've created and measure how long it takes them to reach the floor using the stopwatch. Record this data on the same note paper you've been using the last two weeks.

5. Next, place the spheres into the top of the track one at a time and give them a little push down the ramp. Measure how long it takes them to reach the floor using the stopwatch. Record this data on your note paper.

6. After you've recorded all your "little push" times, it's time for the big push! Place each object at the top of the ramp, give it a big push down, and record the time.

7. After you've done three runs for all your spheres (a drop run, a little push run, and a big push run), take a look at your notes and answer the questions below.

8. Once you're done with this experiment, you should keep your racetrack, as we'll use it for some more experiments in the future.

Follow-Up Questions:

1. How did the mass of the spheres impact how much the friction slowed them down?

~~~~~~

~~~~~~

~~~~~~

2. Did friction affect the dropped objects or the pushed objects more? Why do you think that was the case?

~~~~~~

~~~~~~

~~~~~~

YOGA

Please be aware of your environment and be safe at all times. If you cannot do an exercise, just try your best.

1 - Tree Pose: Stay as long as possible. Note: do on one leg then on another.

2 - Down Dog: 10 sec.

3 - Stretching: Stay as long as possible. Note: do on one leg then on another.

6 - Shavasana: 5 min. Note: this pose is very important and provides you with long term benefits. Try not to skip this. Close your eyes and imagine who you want to be and what your goals are! Always think happy thoughts.

5 - Book Pose: 6 sec. Note: Keep your core tight. Legs should be across from your eyes.

4 - Lower Plank: 6 sec. Note: Keep your back straight and body tight.

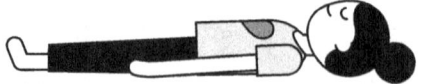

As you read and listen to people talk, it's important to understand exactly what they're expressing. One of the easiest ways people get tripped up is they misunderstand how sure something is. For example, there's a big difference between "Mikey might have the flu" and "Mikey has a serious case of the flu." Let's talk about words you can watch out for as you read and listen to ensure you're understanding how certain a situation is.

Key Terms

Complete Certainty: Perfect knowledge that something is true, accurate, or factual

Strong Certainty: Knowledge that something is most likely to be true or fairly certain to happen

Partial Certainty: Belief or knowledge that something could reasonably happen

Uncertainty: Belief or hope that something might be true or may happen without any proof to back it up

For Example...

Felicia will definitely do well on the test because she pays attention in class, she studied hard, and she has already gotten very high grades on all the previous tests.

> This person is expressing complete certainty that Felicia will do well. The word "definitely" is an indicator. The author also provided several examples of good reasons why they were certain she would succeed.

I assume Felicia will do well on the test because she is a strong student and always comes to class prepared.

> This person is expressing strong certainty that Felicia will do well. The phrase "I assume Felicia will do well" shows that the author believes she is most likely going to succeed. Like the sentence that expressed complete certainty, this author provided examples.

Felicia could do well on the test because she pays attention in class.

Felicia might do well on the test because she pays attention in class.

> These people are expressing partial certainty that Felicia will do well. The words "could" and "might" communicate that the person believes Felicia can do well, but they're not choosing words that show they have a large amount of belief or confidence in her.

It's possible that Felicia will do well on the test.

> This person is expressing uncertainty. They admit that Felicia doing well is one thing that could happen, but there's no confidence in the sentence that it probably will happen. Compared to the previous sentences, this one contains no examples or reasons why Felicia will do well, which demonstrates that the author doesn't believe it's a strong possibility.

The Salt Merchant and His Donkey
By Aesop

Back in ancient times, salt was considered extremely valuable - sometimes even more valuable than gold. That's why, one day, a merchant strapped some bags onto his donkey and went down to the seashore, hoping to get salt at a good price so he could increase his profits selling it to the people who lived inland. When he got to the seashore, the merchant filled his donkey's bags with salt, and he even bought more bags so the donkey could carry twice as much salt as he'd been originally planning.

On the walk home, the merchant and the donkey came to a place where they had to cross a stream. The merchant waded through just fine, but the donkey was so heavy with salt that it stumbled and dumped most of the valuable cargo into the water, where it was washed away. The merchant, extremely frustrated with the situation and the donkey, rode back to the seashore and bought even more salt than the first time.

When the merchant and the donkey returned to the same stream where the donkey had stumbled the first time, the donkey fell on purpose, spilling the extra salt so it was only carrying an amount that it was comfortable with. This time, the merchant realized what the donkey was doing, though, so he formed a new plan.

The merchant returned to the seashore again, but instead of salt, he bought huge bags full of sponges. He brought the donkey back to the stream, where it stumbled on purpose again to try and lighten its load. This time, however, the sponges in the donkey's bags became filled with water, making his load even heavier.

After that, the donkey never questioned how much salt his master gave him to carry.

1. How would you describe the donkey in this story?

~~~~~~

~~~~~~

2. How are the merchant's reactions to the donkey's first stumble and the donkey's second stumble different? Why?

~~~~~~

~~~~~~

3. Which key phrase helped you feel certain as a reader that the donkey's stumbling was not an accident?

    A. "Twice as much salt..." (Paragraph 1)
    B. "The donkey was so heavy with salt..." (Paragraph 2)
    C. "...on purpose..." (Paragraph 3)
    D. "...the amount that it was comfortable with..." (Paragraph 3)

4. Which of these statements can we be certain is true?

    A. The merchant in the story is always mean to his donkey.
    B. The donkey in the story is always lazy and disobedient.
    C. The merchant in the story is already fairly rich
    D. The donkey would've carried the salt if the merchant would've been nicer to him.

5. What is one other way the merchant could have solved his problem?

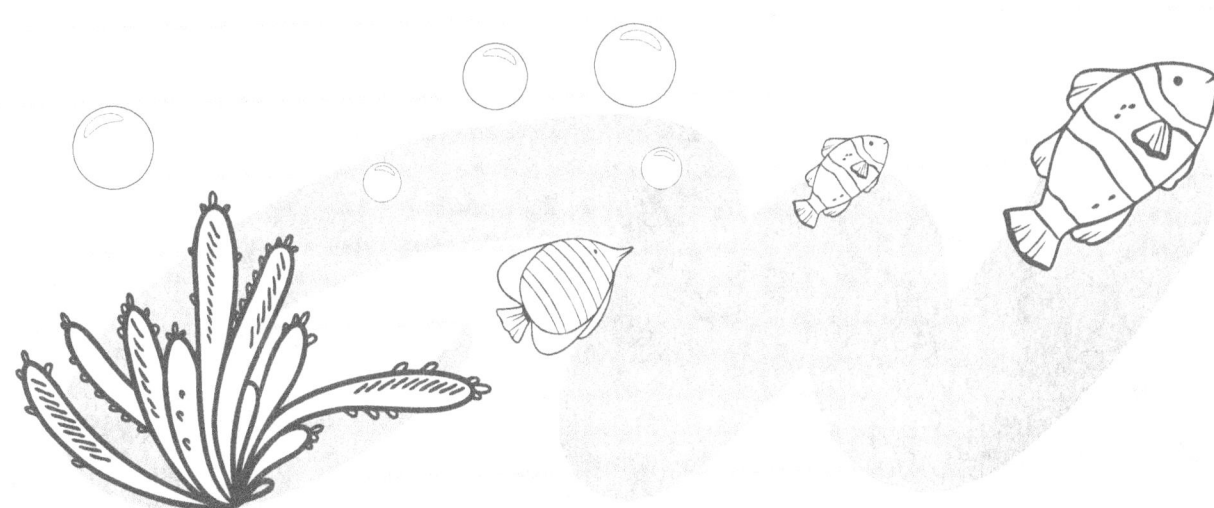

Comparing Degrees of Certainty

Directions:

Read each pair of sentences, then circle the sentence that expresses a **greater degree of certainty** and underline the words in both sentences that served as hints or helped you come up with your answer.

1. My older brother might be on the middle school soccer team this year because he is planning on trying out.

   My older sister is probably going to be on the middle school basketball team this year because she's the best shooter in her grade.

2. We're hoping to get rid of the mice in our house by getting a cat and setting some traps.

   We're calling an exterminator to help us with our mouse problem, so it should be over soon.

3. Ms. Fischer will definitely give us math homework tonight because we learned a new concept in class.

   It's highly likely we'll have to do jumping jacks in P.E. today because they're Mr. Lee's favorite.

4. I assume Monty has gone to the museum before because I know his parents and brother have been there.

   I think it's possible that I'll get invited to Jenna's birthday party.

5. There must be some important differences between alligators and crocodiles, or they wouldn't be considered two different animals.

   I believe one of the differences between alligators and crocodiles involves the shape of their snouts.

FITNESS

Please be aware of your environment and be safe at all times. If you cannot do an exercise, just try your best.

Repeat these **exercises 3 ROUNDS**

2 - Lunges: 2 times to each leg.
Note: Use your body weight or books as weight to do leg lunges.

4 - Run: 50m
Note: Run 25 meters to one side and 25 meters back to the starting position.

1 - Abs: 3 times

3 - Plank: 6 sec.

Two Great Painters
By James Baldwin

There was once a painter whose name was Zeuxis. He could paint pictures so life-like that they were mistaken for the real things which they represented.

At one time he painted the picture of some fruit which was so real that the birds flew down and pecked at it. This made him very proud of his skill.

"I am the only man in the world who can paint a picture so true to life," he said.

There was another famous artist whose name was Parrhasius. When he heard of the boast which Zeuxis had made, he said to himself, "I will see what I can do."

So he painted a beautiful picture which seemed to be covered with a curtain. Then he invited Zeuxis to come and see it.

Zeuxis looked at it closely. "Draw the curtain aside and show us the picture," he said.

Parrhasius laughed and answered, "The curtain is the picture."

"Well," said Zeuxis, "you have beaten me this time, and I shall boast no more. I deceived only the birds, but you have deceived me, a painter."

Some time after this, Zeuxis painted another wonderful picture. It was that of a boy carrying a basket of ripe red cherries. When he hung this painting outside of his door, some birds flew down and tried to carry the cherries away.

"Ah! this picture is a failure," he said. "For if the boy had been as well painted as the cherries, the birds would have been afraid to come near him."

1. How is the "certainty" of birds important to this story?

~~~~~~

~~~~~~

2. How are Zeuxis' and Parrhasius' personalities different from one another?

~~~~~~

~~~~~~

~~~~~~

3. How confident is Zeuxis in his own abilities at the beginning of the story?

   A. Completely Certain
   B. Strong Certainty
   C. Partial Certainty
   D. Uncertain

4. How confident is Parrhasius in his ability to outdo Zeuxis at the beginning of the story?

   A. Complete Certainty
   B. Strong Certainty
   C. Partial Certainty
   D. Uncertain

5. How did Zeuxis' over-certainty in his talents actually lead to his confidence going down?

 Directions:

Fill each blank with one of the words from the bank below to make the sentence express the degree of certainty listed in the parentheses after it.

MAYBE   DEFINITELY   PROBABLY

HOPEFULLY   COULD

1. Our dog Samantha will _____ live at least ten more years, but there's no way to be sure. (UNCERTAINTY)

2. _____ Grandma and Grandpa will come to our house for Thanksgiving Dinner because we went to their place last year. (PARTIAL CERTAINTY)

3. I _____ get a big hit in today's baseball game because I did great at practice this week. (PARTIAL CERTAINTY)

4. We will _____ go to the picnic because we've been looking forward to it all month. (STRONG CERTAINTY)

5. Green is _____ my favorite color of all time. (COMPLETE CERTAINTY)

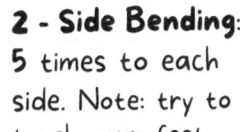 FITNESS

Please be aware of your environment and be safe at all times. If you cannot do an exercise, just try your best.

Repeat these **exercises 3 ROUNDS**

2 - Side Bending: 5 times to each side. Note: try to touch your feet.

1 - Squats: 5 times.
Note: imagine you are trying to sit on a chair.

3 - Tree Pose: Stay as long as possible. Note: do the same with the other leg.

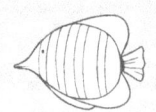

Tables/Charts and understanding data

The chart below shows how many yards Sam ran on some days. Answer questions 1 - 2, using the following data.

Day	Yards Ran
Monday	732
Tuesday	540
Wednesday	658
Thursday	830

1. Which day did Sam run the fewest yards?

   A. Monday
   B. Tuesday
   C. Wednesday
   D. Thursday

2. How many yards did Sam run on Wednesday and Thursday in total?

   A. 1,272
   B. 1,198
   C. 1,370
   D. 1,488

Jules looked in the fridge and found some tomatoes, onions, and lemons. She made a chart to log the food she found.

Food			
How many?	18	10	6

Answer questions 3 - 4, using the data above.

3. Out of the three items in the fridge, which item was the lowest in quantity?

   A. Tomatoes
   B. Onions
   C. Lemons
   D. They are all equal

4. How many more tomatoes were there than lemons?

   A. 12
   B. 8
   C. 6
   D. 4

Bar graph & Line graph

Use the following bar graph to answer questions 1 - 2.

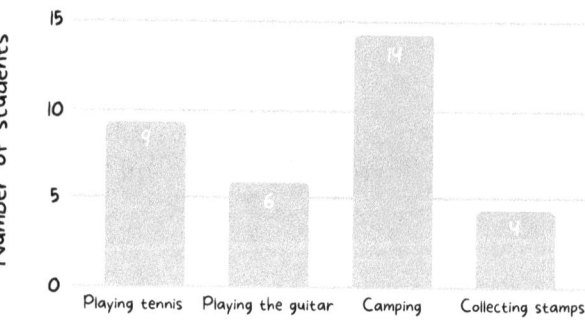

Students' Hobbies

1. How many students were surveyed in total?

   A. 26
   B. 29
   C. 31
   D. 33

2. Which hobby is the most popular?

   Answer _____

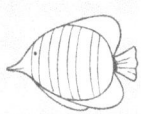

Some friends found seashells on the beach and recorded their quantity. Using the data from the bar graph, answer questions 3 - 4.

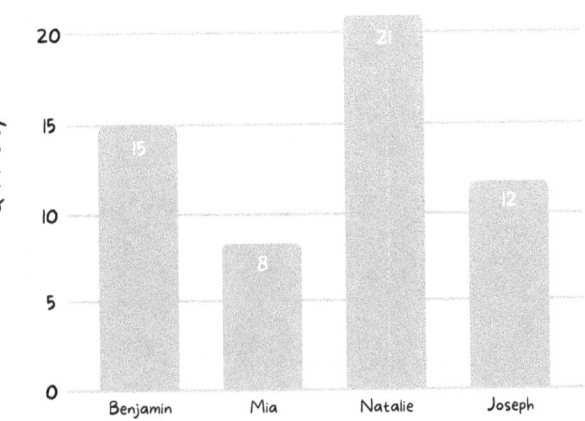

Quantity of Seashells

3. Which friend found the most seashells?

A. Benjamin
B. Mia
C. Natalie
D. Joseph

4. How many more seashells did Natalie find than Mia?

A. 15
B. 13
C. 8
D. 7

FITNESS

Repeat these
exercises
3 ROUNDS

Please be aware of your environment and be safe at all times. If you cannot do an exercise, just try your best.

1 - Bend forward: 10 times. Note: try to touch your feet. Make sure to keep your back straight and if needed you can bend your knees.

2 - Lunges: 3 times to each leg. Note: Use your body weight or books as weight to do leg lunges.

3 - Plank: 6 sec.

4 - Abs: 10 times

Bar graph & Line graph

Stacy graphed the yards she walked during **6** days. Using the data from the bar graph, answer questions 1 - 2.

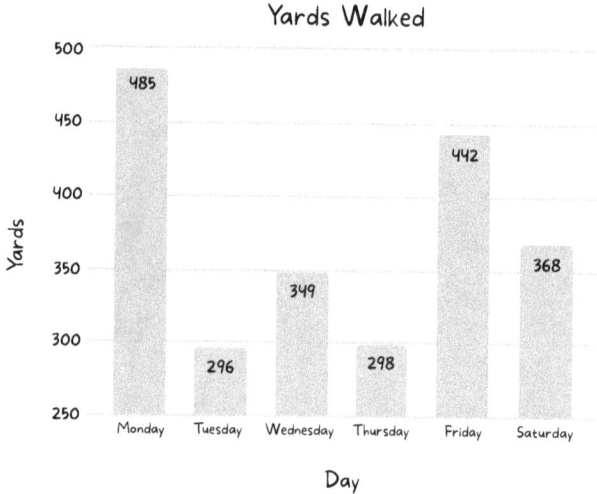

Yards Walked

1. How many yards did Stacy walk on Monday, Thursday and Saturday in total?

   A. 1,151
   B. 1,132
   C. 1,234
   D. 986

2. How many more yards did she walk on Friday than on Tuesday?

   A. 137
   B. 126
   C. 146
   D. 158

The number of pictures that Harold drew during **7** weeks is shown on the bar graph below. Using the data from the bar graph, answer questions 3 - 4

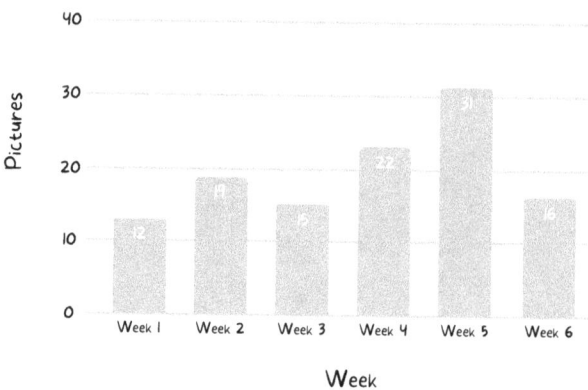

Drawn Pictures

3. How many more pictures did Harold draw on week **5** than week **4**?

   A. 6
   B. 8
   C. 9
   D. 10

4. How many pictures were drawn on weeks 1, 2, 3 and 6 in all?

   A. 56
   B. 62
   C. 67
   D. 58

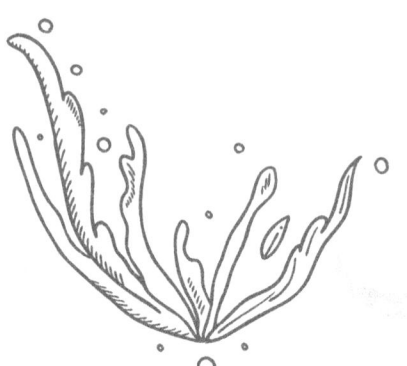

WEEK 5 DAY 4 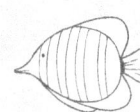 MATH

The bar graph below shows the number of basketball courts in each park. Use the following bar graph to answer questions 5 - 6.

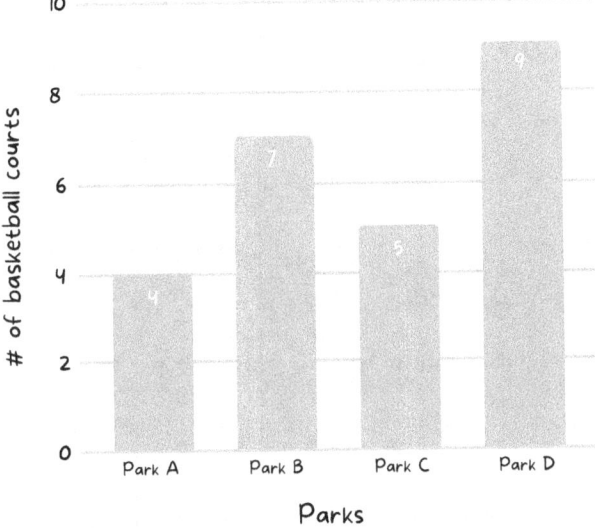

# of basketball courts in parks

(y-axis: # of basketball courts — 0, 2, 4, 6, 8, 10)

Park A: 4
Park B: 7
Park C: 5
Park D: 9

(x-axis: Parks)

5. Which park has the most basketball courts?

   A. Park A
   B. Park B
   C. Park C
   D. Park D

6. How many more basketball courts are at Parks C and D than at Parks A and B?

   Answer _____

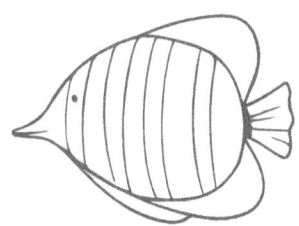

FITNESS

Repeat these **exercises 3 ROUNDS**

Please be aware of your environment and be safe at all times. If you cannot do an exercise, just try your best.

1 - High Plank: 6 sec.

2 - Chair: 10 sec. Note: sit on an imaginary chair, keep your back straight.

3 - Waist Hooping: 10 times. Note: if you do not have a hoop, pretend you have an imaginary hoop and rotate your hips 10 times.

4 - Abs: 10 times

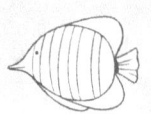

Line of symmetry

1. How many lines of symmetry does this shape have?

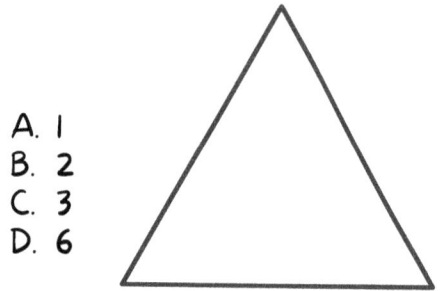

   A. 1
   B. 2
   C. 3
   D. 6

2. Which shape appears to have EXACTLY 1 line of symmetry?

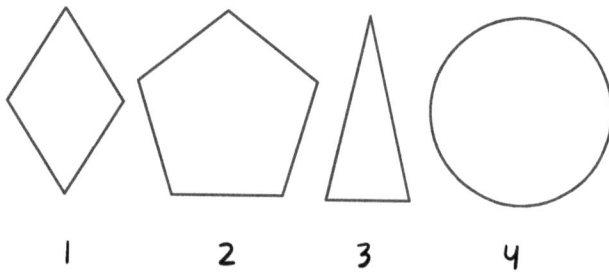

   1   2   3   4

   A. 1
   B. 2
   C. 3
   D. 4

3. Draw all the lines of symmetry for this shape.

4. In the shape below, which of the following is a line of symmetry?

   A. AB
   B. CD
   C. EF
   D. YZ

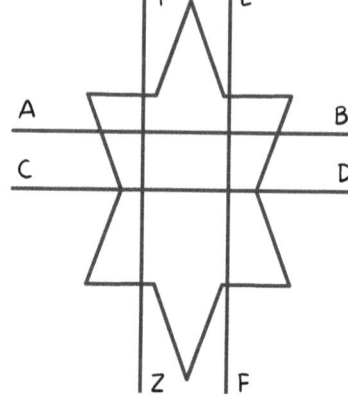

5. Is this shape symmetrical? How do you know?

   Answer _____

6. Which object appears to have more than 1 line of symmetry?

   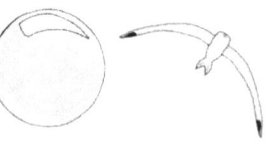

   1   2   3   4

   A. 1
   B. 2
   C. 3
   D. 4

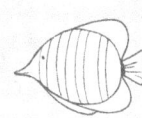

7. Draw all the lines of symmetry for this object.

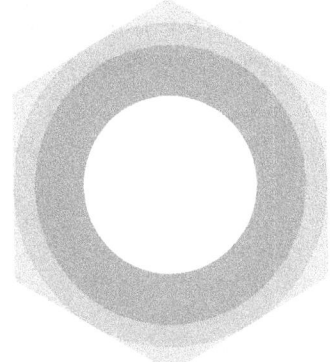

8. How many lines of symmetry does this object have?

A. 1
B. 4
C. 8
D. 16

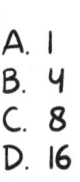

9. Which object has EXACTLY 4 lines of symmetry?

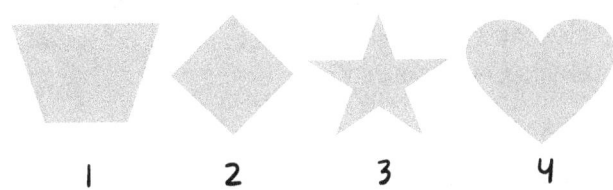

1   2   3   4

A. 1
B. 2
C. 3
D. 4

10. How many lines of symmetry does this shape have?

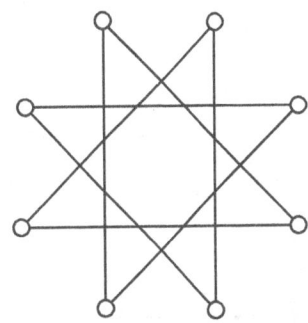

Answer _____

Please be aware of your environment and be safe at all times. If you cannot do an exercise, just try your best.

1 - Down Dog: 10 sec.

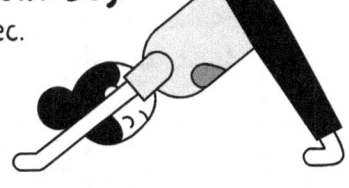

2 - Bend Down: 10 sec.

3 - Chair: 10 sec.

4 - Child Pose: 20 sec.

5 - Shavasana: as long as you can. Note: think of happy moments and relax your mind.

WEEK 5 DAY 6 EXPERIMENT

Comparing Magnetic Force

When we made our racetrack, we said **force** was a push or a pull that impacts an object's **motion**. One kind of **force** we can observe in everyday life is magnetism. Magnets have a **charge** that might attract, repel, or have no effect at all on objects, depending on what those objects are made from.

Materials:

- An assortment of household magnets, such as...
  - Refrigerator magnets
  - Disc magnets
  - Bar magnets
  - Any handheld tools with magnets on them (flashlights, screwdrivers, etc.)
- A variety of small metal objects, such as...
  - Staples
  - Paper clips
  - Coins
  - Scissors
  - Keys
  - Screws or nails
- Note paper

Procedure:

1. Begin by separating out the different kinds of magnets you have and briefly describe each one on your note paper. Describe what the magnet **looks like**, what it **feels like**, and how **big it is**. After you've looked at all the magnets, make some predictions about which ones you think will be the **best or strongest** and why.

2. Arrange your small metal objects on a tabletop, and **slowly move the magnet near and around each one**. On your note sheet, keep track of which objects the magnet can **pick up**, which objects the magnet can **stick to**, and which objects the magnet **seemingly has no effect on**. As you go, think about which magnets are working the best and which ones are the weakest.

3. Once you've tested all your magnets, clear the table and set all the small metal objects aside.

4. Next, test to **see how your different magnets interact with each other**. (**NOTE:** Be careful as you do this, as some magnets might want to stick together or force each other apart stronger than you are expecting!) Take two different magnets and bring them close to each other, rotating them to see how all sides interact with each other. Observe whether they seem to want to stick together, force apart, or have no interaction at all, and **write the results on your note paper**. Repeat this process until you've compared all the magnets.

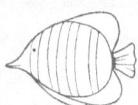

5. Answer the questions below and **gather up your materials**. You'll want to use these same magnets and metal objects for next week's experiment.

Follow-Up Questions:

1. What did you learn about some of the different kinds of magnets you have around your house? Which ones were **able to do things the other magnets couldn't?**

2. Did you have any metal objects that the magnets couldn't pick up? Which ones were they?

YOGA

Please be aware of your environment and be safe at all times. If you cannot do an exercise, just try your best.

1 - Tree Pose: Stay as long as possible. Note: do on one leg then on another.

2 - Down Dog: 10 sec.

3 - Stretching: Stay as long as possible. Note: do on one leg then on another.

6 - Shavasana: 5 min. Note: this pose is very important and provides you with long term benefits. Try not to skip this. Close your eyes and imagine who you want to be and what your goals are! Always think happy thoughts.

4 - Lower Plank: 6 sec. Note: Keep your back straight and body tight.

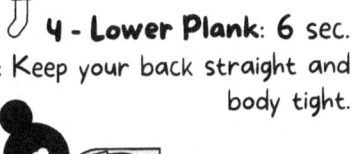

5 - Book Pose: 6 sec. Note: Keep your core tight. Legs should be across from your eyes.

99

WEEK 5 DAY 7 🐟 MAZE

Task: Help Amy the astronaut find the correct way to the rocket. Color in the pathway so Amy the astronaut can take off!

Are you having fun learning new concepts?
Learning should always be fun! We tend to remember more information when we enjoy the learning experience.

WEEK 6

It's a goldfish!
You have probably seen this creature since the goldfish is the most popular aquarium fish. Here's a fun fact: A goldfish can see more colors than a human!

As you begin to read more advanced texts, you'll find that people sometimes use words to represent something other than their basic meaning. We call that **figurative language**. Identifying figurative language in texts you read, while also introducing it to your own writing, shows that you are a master of language!

Key Terms

Literal Meaning: The most basic level of language, where the focus is on being clear and communicating basic meaning

Figurative Language: Using comparisons, analogies, or other tricks of language to make writing more descriptive and less literal

Basic Forms of Figurative Language:

Type of Fig. Language	Definition	Example
Simile	A comparison between two things that uses either the word **like** or **as**.	Ms. Hutchins is wise **like** an owl. OR She is **as** fast **as** a cheetah on the basketball court.
Metaphor	A comparison between two things that does <u>not</u> use like or as.	Ms. Hutchins **is** a wise old owl. OR She **is** a sprinting cheetah on the basketball court.
Personification	Describing an object or animal as though it has human qualities.	The wind **pulled** at my hair and **whispered** into my ear with its cold **breath**.
Hyperbole	Exaggerating or over-stating something to make a point.	Our air conditioning is broken, so it is **like a thousand degrees** in our house.

Focusing on literal meaning is really important to make sure you're choosing words that communicate ideas clearly. However, figurative language provides you more opportunities to be creative.

For Example...

- Jennifer is a very tall person.

Can become...

- Jennifer is **like** a giant squeezing into a toy car when she gets in her family's vehicle. (SIMILE)
- Jennifer **is a giraffe** living in a world of ants. (METAPHOR)
- Jennifer is so tall that **lamp posts get jealous** of her. (PERSONIFICATION)
- When you first meet her, it's easy to think Jennifer is **at least eight feet tall**. (HYPERBOLE)

The Thief and the Innkeeper
By Aesop

A thief checked into a hotel room that he knew he couldn't pay for, but he planned to steal something valuable to pay for the room before the time he checked out. After a few days at the inn, the thief was worried because he hadn't found anything worth enough money to pay for his room. He began to notice that the innkeeper had a very nice new coat, though, and he thought that if he could get ahold of that, he might be able to cover the bill.

The thief sat down with the innkeeper and started a long, rambling conversation about all sorts of different topics. After he'd talked the innkeeper's ear off for several hours, the thief started making big yawning noises. As he yawned, he would occasionally also howl like a wolf. After a few minutes of this, the innkeeper was very disturbed.

"Why are you howling like a wolf?" he asked.

"I will tell you," the thief said, "but first hold onto my clothes. When I get these yawning attacks, I turn into a wolf and attack people. The worst part is that my clothes get completely torn up and ruined every time."

The innkeeper was very nervous as the thief handed him his jacket and socks, but it only got worse when the thief began yawning and howling again.

"Please, take my clothes!" the thief begged. "I'm about to turn into a wolf!"

The innkeeper screamed in fear and ran out of the room. Not only did he leave the thief's clothes behind, he also forgot to grab his beautiful new coat, which the thief snatched as he walked out the door.

The moral of the story: Not every tale should be believed.

1. What is the thief's original plan when he checks into the hotel room?

2. How is what happens at the end of the story different from the thief's original plan?

3. What kind of figurative language is used in the phrase "...howl like a wolf?"

   A. Simile
   B. Metaphor
   C. Personification
   D. Hyperbole

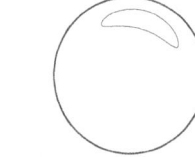

4. Which of these phrases from the passage contains **figurative language?**

   A. "He planned to steal something valuable to pay for the room..."
   B. "The thief started making big yawning noises..."
   C. "After he'd talked the innkeeper's ear off for several hours..."
   D. "It only got worse when the thief began yawning and howling again..."

5. How could the thief have approached this situation in an honest way? Give one or two examples:

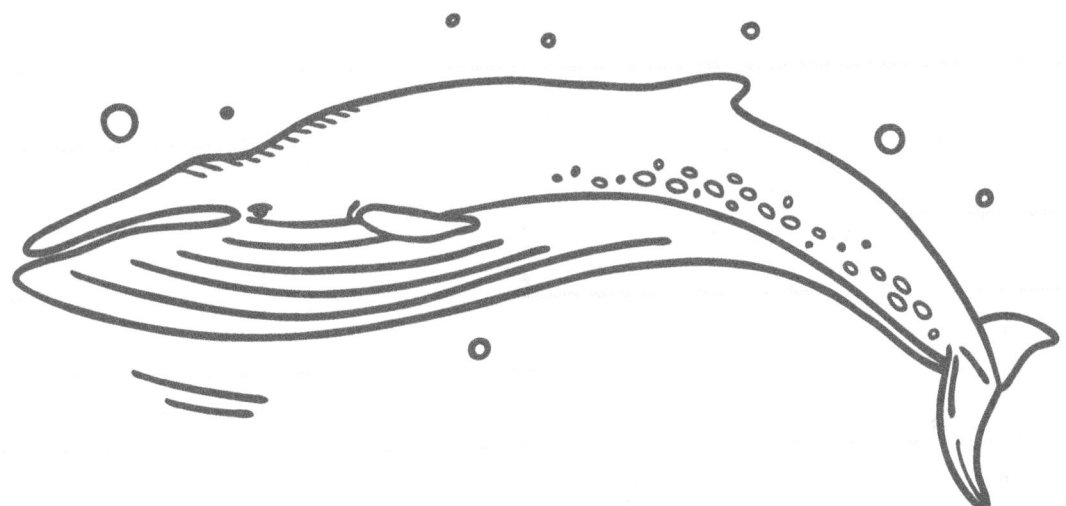

WEEK 6 DAY 1

Identifying Basic Forms of Figurative Language

 Directions:

Underline the example of figurative language in each sentence and then write whether it is an example of a **simile, metaphor, personification, or hyperbole.**

1. I was hoping to go for a run outside, but of course it turned out to be the crummiest day of the whole year.

2. Our dog is a monster when it comes to food.

3. My smartphone is my best friend because it helps me get the information I need, and I can play games on it.

4. The sun was so hot I felt like an egg frying in a pan.

5. Mrs. Turner is the strictest principal in the history of school.

FITNESS

Please be aware of your environment and be safe at all times. If you cannot do an exercise, just try your best.

Repeat these **exercises 3 ROUNDS**

2 - Lunges: 2 times to each leg.
Note: Use your body weight or books as weight to do leg lunges.

4 - Run: 50m
Note: Run 25 meters to one side and **25** meters back to the starting position.

3 - Plank: 6 sec.

1 - Abs: 3 times

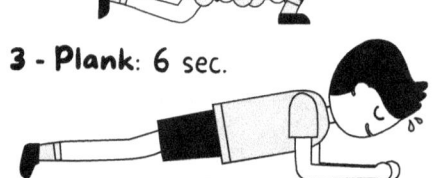

The Surly Guest
By James Baldwin

One day John Randolph, of Roanoke, set out on horseback to ride to a town that was many miles from his home. The road was strange to him, and he traveled very slowly.

When night came on he stopped at a pleasant roadside inn and asked for lodging. The innkeeper welcomed him kindly. He had often heard of the great John Randolph, and therefore he did all that he could to entertain him well.

A fine supper was prepared, and the innkeeper himself waited upon his guest. John Randolph ate in silence. The innkeeper spoke of the weather, of the roads, of the crops, of politics. But his surly guest said scarcely a word.

In the morning a good breakfast was served, and then Mr. Randolph made ready to start on his journey. He called for his bill and paid it. His horse was led to the door, and a servant helped him to mount it.

As he was starting away, the friendly innkeeper said, "Which way will you travel, Mr. Randolph?"

Mr. Randolph looked at him in no gentle way, and answered, "Sir!"

"I only asked which way you intend to travel," said the man.

"Oh! Have I paid you my bill?"

"Yes, sir."

"Do I owe you anything more?"

"No, sir."

"Then, I intend to travel the way I wish to go, do you understand?"

He turned his horse and rode away. He had not gone farther than to the end of the innkeeper's field, when to his surprise he found that the road forked. He did not know whether he should take the right-hand fork or the left-hand.

He paused for a while. There was no signboard to help him. He looked back and saw the innkeeper still standing by the door. He called to him: "My friend, which of these roads shall I travel to go to Lynchburg?"

"Mr. Randolph," answered the innkeeper, "you have paid your bill and don't owe me a cent. Travel the way you wish to go. Good-bye!"

As bad luck would have it, Mr. Randolph took the wrong road. He went far out of his way and lost much time, all on account of his surliness.

1. Based on the passage, what are some other words that mean the same thing (or close to the same thing) as surly?

2. How is the **figurative meaning** of Mr. Randolph's question "Do I owe you anything more?" different from the **literal meaning** of his words?

3. Which description early in the story is later proven to be false or incorrect?

   A. "...a pleasant roadside inn..."
   B. "...welcomed him kindly..."
   C. "...the great John Randolph..."
   D. "...a fine supper..."

4. Which of these phrases from the passage contains **figurative language**?

   A. "The innkeeper spoke of the weather..."
   B. "...he found out that the road forked."
   C. "There was no signboard to help him..."
   D. "He went far out of his way and lost much time..."

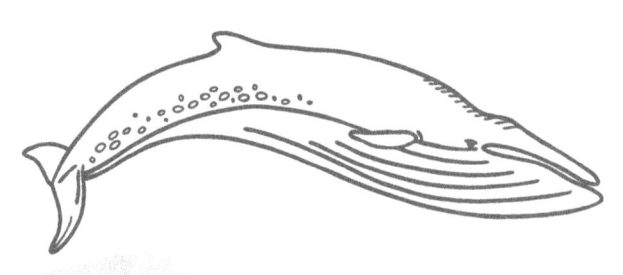

5. Create **three** similes or metaphors that could describe **John Randolph**. Then, create **three** similes or metaphors that could describe the **Innkeeper**.

John Randolph:

Innkeeper:

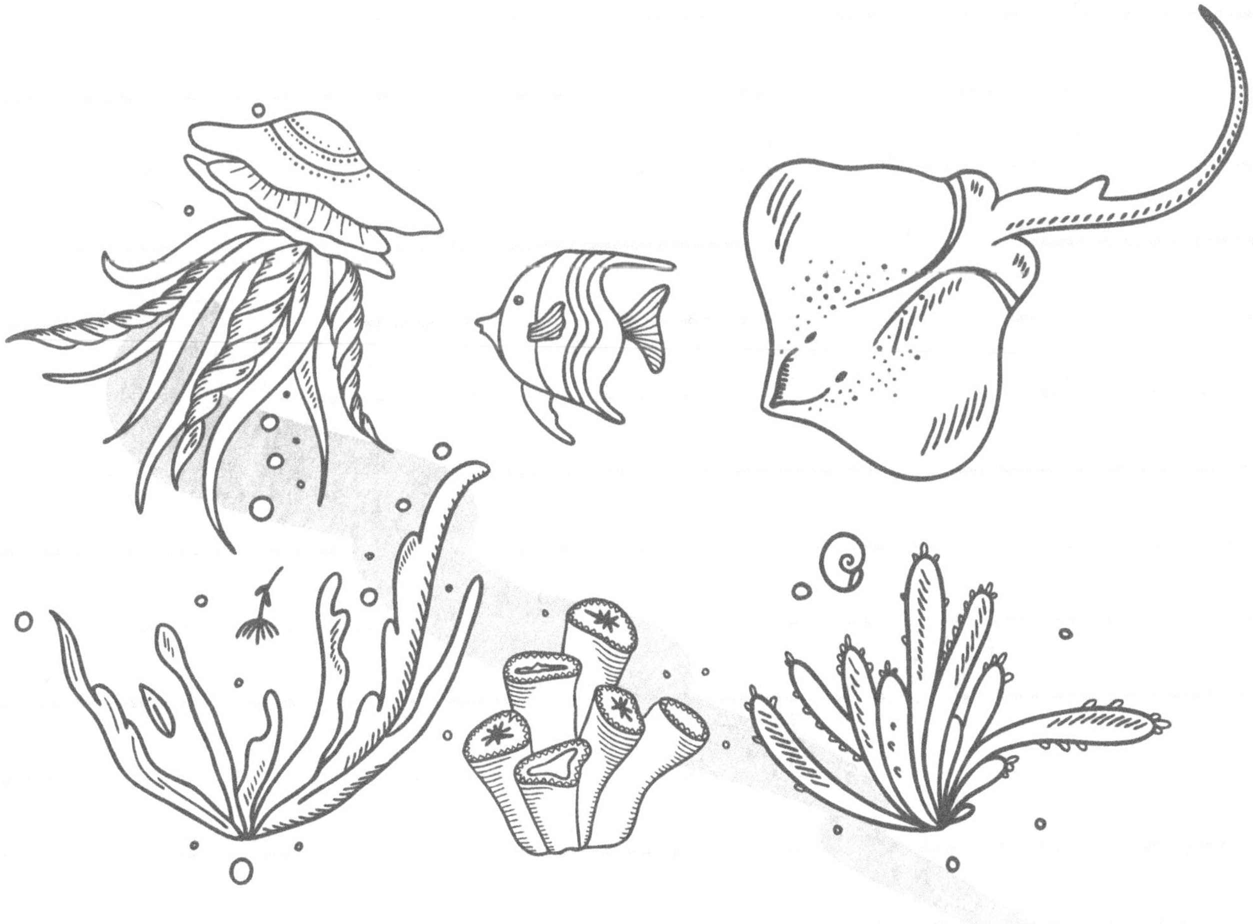

WEEK 6 DAY 2  ACTIVITIES
LITERAL VS. FIGURATIVE LANGUAGE

 Directions:

Complete the sentences by adding your own examples of figurative language as described in the parentheses.

1. Trevor is _____ when he runs.

    (Create a SIMILE about how FAST Trevor is)

2. My cousin Francine is _____

    _____

    (Create a METAPHOR about how SMART Francine is)

3. The first time I ever saw a horror movie, I thought I was going to _____

    _____ .

    (Use HYPERBOLE to describe how SCARED you were by the movie)

4. The bicycle _____

    _____ which made the rider fall.

    (Use PERSONIFICATION to describe how the BICYCLE made the rider fall)

5. I created a painting that was _____

    _____ in art class last week.

    (Create a SIMILE about how COLORFUL the painting is)

FITNESS

Please be aware of your environment and be safe at all times. If you cannot do an exercise, just try your best.

Repeat these **exercises 3 ROUNDS**

1 - Squats: 5 times.
Note: imagine you are trying to sit on a chair.

2 - Side Bending: 5 times to each side. Note: try to touch your feet.

3 - Tree Pose: Stay as long as possible. Note: do the same with the other leg.

WEEK 6 DAY 3  MATH

Identifying perpendicular lines, parallel lines, points, lines and rays.

Use the drawing below to answer questions 1 - 2.

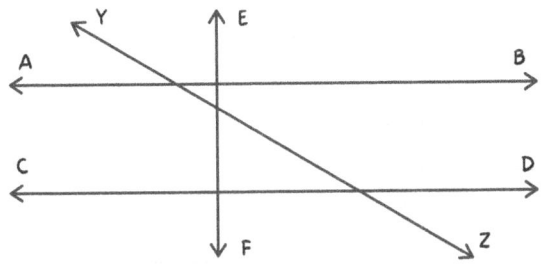

1. Which lines are parallel?

   A. AB and CD
   B. AB and EF
   C. EF and YZ
   D. CD and YZ

2. Which lines are perpendicular?

   A. AB and CD
   B. AB and EF
   C. EF and YZ
   D. CD and YZ

Use the drawing below to answer questions 3 - 4.

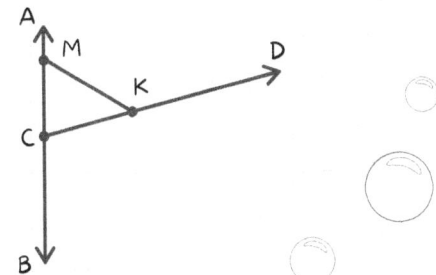

3. Which of the following answer choices is a line?

   A. AB
   B. CD
   C. MK
   D. CK

4. Which of the following answer choices is a ray?

   A. AB
   B. CD
   C. MK
   D. CK

Use the drawing below to answer questions 5 - 6.

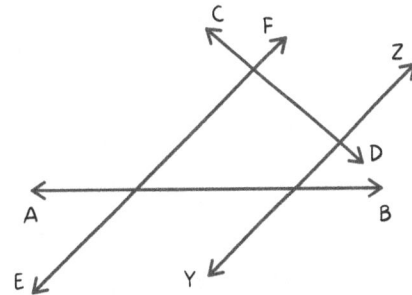

5. Which lines are perpendicular?

   A. AB and CD
   B. AB and EF
   C. EF and YZ
   D. CD and YZ

6. Which lines are parallel?

   A. AB and CD
   B. AB and EF
   C. EF and YZ
   D. CD and YZ

Use the drawing below to answer questions 7 - 8.

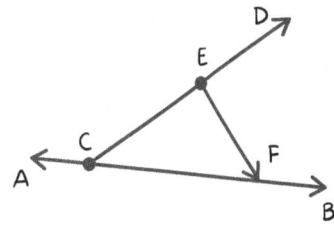

7. What is CD?

   A. A line
   B. A line segment
   C. A ray
   D. A point

8. What is E?

   A. A line
   B. A line segment
   C. A ray
   D. A point

9. How many rays are in the drawing?

   A. 1
   B. 2
   C. 3
   D. 4

10. How many lines are in the drawing?

   A. 1
   B. 2
   C. 3
   D. 4

Use the drawing below to answer questions 9 - 10.

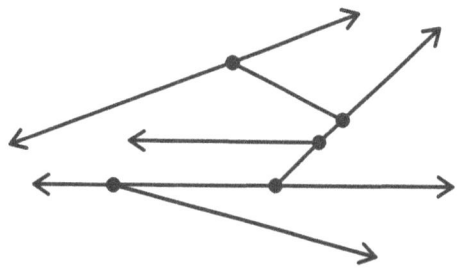

FITNESS

Please be aware of your environment and be safe at all times. If you cannot do an exercise, just try your best.

Repeat these exercises **3 ROUNDS**

1 - Bend forward: 10 times.
Note: try to touch your feet. Make sure to keep your back straight and if needed you can bend your knees.

2 - Lunges: 3 times to each leg.
Note: Use your body weight or books as weight to do leg lunges.

4 - Abs: 10 times

3 - Plank: 6 sec.

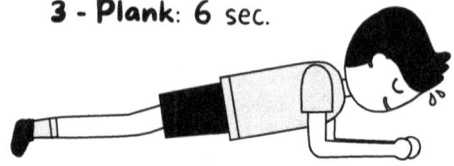

WEEK 6 DAY 4  MATH

Time

1. What time is represented on the clock below?

   A. Thirty-seven five
   B. Five forty
   C. Forty four
   D. Four thirty-eight

2. What time does the clock show?

   A. 1:53
   B. 12:43
   C. 12:53
   D. 1:50

3. What time will it be in one hour and twenty-five minutes?

   A. 3:55
   B. 4:30
   C. 4:35
   D. 4:25

4. Look at the digital clock:

   Which analog clock shows the same time?

   A. 1
   B. 2
   C. 3
   D. 4

5. Mrs. Clark is cooking breakfast. The clock shows:

   What time is it?

   A. 6:23 am
   B. 7:23 am
   C. 6:23 pm
   D. 7:23 pm

6. What is the elapsed time between the two times represented on the clocks below?

   Answer _____

7. Trish is going to the gym in 2 and a half hours. It is now 2:45 pm. What time is Trish going to the gym?

   Answer _____

8. Jim is eating soup for lunch. The clock shows:

   What time is it?

   A. 2:50 am
   B. 3:50 am
   C. 2:50 pm
   D. 3:50 pm

9. What is another way to write 1:12 pm in words?

   Answer _____

10. What is the elapsed time between 10:55 am and 2:18 pm?

Answer _____

Unit conversions (minutes, seconds, hours, liters, etc)

1. How many seconds are in 7 minutes?

   A. 360 seconds
   B. 380 seconds
   C. 420 seconds
   D. 480 seconds

2. Which of the following completes the equation?

5,700 grams = ____ kilograms + ____ grams

   Answer _____

3. If a bag of sugar weighs about 3 kilograms, how many grams does the bag of sugar weigh?

   A. 30 grams
   B. 30,000 grams
   C. 3,000 grams
   D. 300 grams

4. Which symbol makes the following inequality TRUE?

   7 liters _____ 560 ml.

   A. >
   B. <
   C. =
   D. +

5. How many minutes are in 4 hours?

   A. 180 minutes
   B. 120 minutes
   C. 220 minutes
   D. 240 minutes

6. How many milliliters are in 8 liters?

   A. 8,000 mL
   B. 800 mL
   C. 80 mL
   D. 8 mL

7. Convert: 48 hours = ____ days.

   Answer _____

8. Find 136 cm subtracted from 3 m.

   Answer _____

Please be aware of your environment and be safe at all times. If you cannot do an exercise, just try your best.

FITNESS

Repeat these exercises **3 ROUNDS**

3 - Waist Hooping: 10 times.
Note: if you do not have a hoop, pretend you have an imaginary hoop and rotate your hips 10 times.

1 - High Plank: 6 sec.

2 - Chair: 10 sec.
Note: sit on an imaginary chair, keep your back straight.

4 - Abs: 10 times

WEEK 6 DAY 5  MATH

Word problems for unit conversions

1. Hannah has **3** containers that each have **3** liters of water in them. How many milliliters of water does Hannah have in total?

   A. **9** mL
   B. **90** mL
   C. **900** mL
   D. **9,000** mL

2. Mike has five bags of potatoes that each weigh **6,000** grams. How many kilograms of potatoes does he have?

   A. **3** kilograms
   B. **30** kilograms
   C. **300** kilograms
   D. **3,000** kilograms

3. Roger spends **17** minutes to get to his school. How many seconds does it take for him to get to school?

   A. **960** seconds
   B. **980** seconds
   C. **1,020** seconds
   D. **1,080** seconds

4. Haley finished studying for her math exam at **5** pm. If her study time was **75** minutes long, what time did she start to study?

   A. **3:45** pm
   B. **3:55** pm
   C. **3:35** pm
   D. **2:55** pm

5. Teddy bought **1,300** grams of flour. How much flour did Teddy buy in kilograms?

   A. **1** kilogram and **100** grams
   B. **1** kilogram and **500** grams
   C. **1** kilogram and **300** grams
   D. **1** kilogram and **600** grams

6. Lilly has five cartons of juice that each contains **800** mL in them. How many liters do the five cartons hold altogether?

   Answer _____

7. Molly weighed her cat. The cat weighed **4** kilograms and **500** grams. Convert this measurement into grams.

   Answer _____

8. Willy's basketball weighs **2,000** grams. What is its weight in kilograms?

   Answer _____

9. There are **9,000** milliliters of apple juice in a container. How many liters are there in all?

   Answer _____

10. Jeffrey enjoys reading magazines. . It was **5:39** pm when he started reading. It took him **86** minutes to read it till the end. What time was it when Jeffrey finished reading the magazine?

    Answer _____

WEEK 6 DAY 5  MATH

Word problems dealing with mass and volume

1. If three buckets below are equal, how much does the second bucket hold?

8 liters   ?   ?

A. 80 milliliters
B. 800 milliliters
C. 8 milliliter
D. 8,000 milliliters

2. How many liters total can the three buckets above hold?

Answer _____

3. There was an aquarium that held 15 liters of water. The cup can hold $\frac{1}{2}$ liter. How many cups do you need to fill the aquarium?

A. 15 cups
B. 20 cups
C. 30 cups
D. 35 cups

4. There are 100 grams of vitamins per bottle. How many grams of vitamins are there in 11 bottles?

Answer _____

5. If one book has a mass of 7 grams, then what is the mass of 17 books?

A. 109 g
B. 119 g
C. 129 g
D. 139 g

Please be aware of your environment and be safe at all times. If you cannot do an exercise, just try your best.

1 - Down Dog: 10 sec.

2 - Bend Down: 10 sec.

3 - Chair: 10 sec.

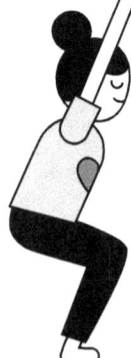

4 - Child Pose: 20 sec.

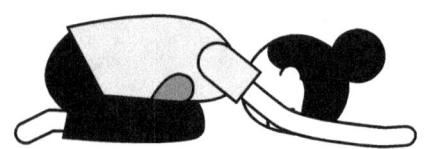

5 - Shavasana: as long as you can. Note: think of happy moments and relax your mind.

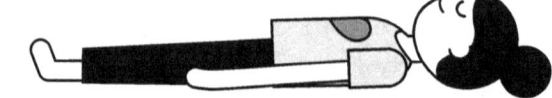

WEEK 6 DAY 6 EXPERIMENT

Using Magnetic Force to Move Objects

Now that we've seen magnetism at work, let's think about how we can use magnets and magnetic force to **create motion**.

Materials:

 Your racetrack (see Week 2's Experiment)

 An assortment of household magnets, such as...
- Refrigerator magnets
- Disc magnets
- Bar magnets
- Any handheld tools with magnets on them (flashlights, screwdrivers, etc.)

 A variety of small metal objects, such as...
- Staples
- Paper clips
- Coins
- Scissors
- Keys
- Screws or nails

 Note paper

Procedure:

1. Set up your racetrack, but instead of propping it up like a ramp, **lay it flat** on a tabletop or floor.

2. Gather your small metal objects. It's ideal if they're the same ones you used last week, but they don't have to be. **NOTE:** If you want, you can use your balance to compare the masses of the objects before you go any further. If you do that, be sure to rank them on your notepaper!

3. Place one of your metal objects at one end of the track. Then, take your **weakest magnet** (based on your notes from last week) and, holding the magnet above the track, see if you can move the metal object down the track by sliding the magnet above it. If you can't move the object at all (or can only pick it up with the magnet without getting the object to move down the track) try a different magnet.

4. **Test all your different metal objects using all your different magnets** and make note of which magnets can effectively move the object down the track and which objects are the easiest for the magnets to move.

5. Answer the questions below, and then put your materials away. **We are officially done with the racetrack for the summer,** but you can keep it for your own future experiments, if you want!

WEEK 6 DAY 6 🐟 EXPERIMENT

Follow-Up Questions:

1. How did this experience show you that the **strongest magnet isn't always the best** tool for every job?

2. Which magnet/metal object pairing did you find was the **easiest to move effectively** down the track? **Why** do you think that combination worked so well?

YOGA

Please be aware of your environment and be safe at all times. If you cannot do an exercise, just try your best.

1 - Tree Pose: Stay as long as possible. Note: do on one leg then on another.

2 - Down Dog: 10 sec.

3 - Stretching: Stay as long as possible. Note: do on one leg then on another.

4 - Lower Plank: 6 sec.
Note: Keep your back straight and body tight.

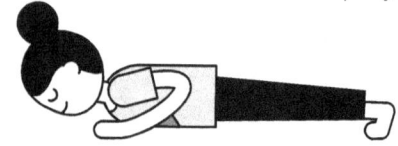

5 - Book Pose: 6 sec.
Note: Keep your core tight. Legs should be across from your eyes.

6 - Shavasana: 5 min.
Note: this pose is very important and provides you with long term benefits. Try not to skip this. Close your eyes and imagine who you want to be and what your goals are! Always think happy thoughts.

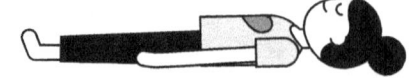

WEEK 6 DAY 7  MAZE

Task: Meet Dinosaurs 1, 2, 3, 4 and 5! Help them match their number with the correct letter (body).

Halfway there!

You have successfully completed half of this workbook. Are you excited to continue learning? I sure am.

WEEK 7

It's a turtle!

Turtles are reptiles that can live over 100 years. Sea turtles in particular have been known to have a lifespan over 150+ years.

WEEK 7 DAY 1  OVERVIEW OF ENGLISH CONCEPTS
FACT VS. OPINION

One crucial skill you need as a reader is the ability to recognize whether what you're reading is **fact** or **opinion**. While this sounds simple at first, it can actually be very tricky because people tend to be very confident in their opinions and present them as though they are facts. However, a little thinking and a little research can quickly help you tell whether what you're reading is indisputably true or just an opinion.

Key Terms

Fact: Something that can be proven as definitely true

Opinion: Something that someone thinks, believes, or hopes is true

When people state their opinion, there are usually words or phrases that serve as **hints** that someone is sharing their **personal perspective**, rather than stating something that is undeniably true. Here are a few of those "watch words" to look out for. If you see any of these, you're reading a statement of **opinion, not fact!**

Words & Phrases that Clearly Indicate Opinion		
I think	I feel	I hope
I believe	In my opinion	From my point of view
It seems to me	I am confident that	My perspective

People don't always use phrases like these, though. In fact, sometimes, people just **present their opinions as though they are facts** to show their confidence and try to convince people to see things their way.

That means that in order to be sure something is **actually a fact**, you need to:

- **Look for evidence**, support, or examples in the sentence that show that something is definitely true

- Ask yourself, "**Could someone disagree with this statement** without necessarily being wrong?"

  - If you can disagree with something without being wrong, that proves it is a fact and not an opinion.

 For Example...

In the sentence...

I believe Mark is the best choice for class president. **(OPINION)**

- The phrase "I believe..." at the beginning tips us off that this is an opinion.

Mark is the best choice for class president. **(OPINION PRESENTED AS FACT)**

- The speaker here never says "I believe," **but** they don't offer any specific evidence to back up their point, and someone could easily disagree with this statement and **not necessarily be wrong**.

Mark is a strong candidate for class president because he is a good student and he communicates very well with his classmates. **(FACT)**

- The speaker avoids being too dramatic about how good a candidate Mark is (they avoid saying he is "the best") and also provides specific pieces of evidence to back up their point of view.

The Apes and the Two Travelers
By Aesop

Two men, one who always spoke the truth and the other who told nothing but lies, were traveling together and by chance came to the land of Apes. One of the Apes, who had raised himself to be king, commanded them to be seized and brought before him, that he might know what was said of him among men.

He ordered at the same time that all the Apes be arranged in a long row on his right hand and on his left, and that a throne be placed for him, as was the custom among men. After these preparations he signified that the two men should be brought before him, and greeted them with this salutation: "What sort of a king do I seem to you to be, O strangers?"

The Lying Traveler replied, "You seem to me a most mighty king."

"And what is your estimate of those you see around me?"

"These," he made answer, "are worthy companions of yourself, fit at least to be ambassadors and leaders of armies."

The Ape and all his court, gratified with the lie, commanded that a handsome present be given to the flatterer. On this the truthful Traveler thought to himself, "If so great a reward be given for a lie, with what gift may not I be rewarded, if, according to my custom, I tell the truth?"

The Ape quickly turned to him. "And pray how do I and these my friends around me seem to you?"

"Thou art," he said, "a most excellent Ape, and all these thy companions after thy example are excellent Apes too." The King of the Apes, enraged at hearing these truths, gave him over to the teeth and claws of his companions.

1. How would you describe the King of the Apes in the story?

2. What happens to the truthful traveler at the end of the story?

3. Which of these statements about the story is a **fact**?

   A. The lying traveler should not have been rewarded
   B. The truthful traveler should not have been punished
   C. The King of the Apes wanted to be flattered
   D. The truthful traveler should have chosen better words

4. Which of these statements about the story is an **opinion**?

   A. The truthful traveler should have lied
   B. The Ape King was quick to punish the truthful traveler
   C. The lying traveler saved his own life by refusing to tell the truth
   D. The lying traveler got a present from the Ape King

5. Based on the story, why can it be harder or more frustrating to focus on **facts**, rather than just sharing an **opinion**?

ACTIVITIES
FACT VS. OPINION

 Directions:

Read each sentence, then write on the line below whether it is **fact** or **opinion**. Once you've done that, circle the words in the sentence that helped you choose your answer.

1. The Boston Red Sox are the best team in the whole world.

2. I know I am sick because I took my temperature and I have a fever of 101 degrees.

3. Ms. Foster is mean because she always gives me lunch detention when I forget my homework.

4. Tiger Woods is one of the most important golfers of all time because he has won more than 105 professional tournaments and has helped the game grow in popularity.

5. Everybody loves Thanksgiving because it is the time of year when families come together to celebrate what they are thankful for, eat a delicious meal, and watch football.

FITNESS

Please be aware of your environment and be safe at all times. If you cannot do an exercise, just try your best.

Repeat these **exercises 3 ROUNDS**

2 - Lunges: 2 times to each leg.
Note: Use your body weight or books as weight to do leg lunges.

4 - Run: 50m
Note: Run 25 meters to one side and 25 meters back to the starting position.

1 - Abs: 3 times

3 - Plank: 6 sec.

The Dark Day
By James Baldwin

Listen, and I will tell you of the famous dark day in Connecticut. It was in the month of May, more than a hundred years ago.

The sun rose bright and fair, and the morning was without a cloud. The air was very still. There was not a breath of wind to stir the young leaves on the trees.

Then, about the middle of the day, it began to grow dark. The sun was hidden. A black cloud seemed to cover the earth.

The birds flew to their nests. The chickens went to roost. The cows came home from the pasture and stood mooing at the gate. It grew so dark that the people could not see their way along the streets.

Then everybody began to feel frightened. "What is the matter? What is going to happen?" each one asked of another. The children cried. The dogs howled. The women wept, and some of the men prayed.

"The end of the world has come!" cried some; and they ran about in the darkness.

"This is the last great day!" cried others; and they knelt down and waited.

In the old statehouse, the wise men of Connecticut were sitting. They were men who made the laws, and much depended upon their wisdom.

When the darkness came, they too began to be alarmed. The gloom was terrible.

"It is the day of the Lord," said one.

"No use to make laws," said another, "for they will never be needed."

"I move that we adjourn," said a third.

Then up from his seat rose Abraham Davenport.

His voice was clear and strong, and all knew that he, at least, was not afraid.

"This may be the last great day," he said. "I do not know whether the end of the world has come or not. But I am sure that it is my duty to stand at my post as long as I live. So, let us go on with the work that is before us. Let the candles be lighted."

His words put courage into every heart. The candles were brought in. Then with his strong face aglow in their feeble light, he made a speech in favor of a law to help poor fishermen.

And as he spoke, the other lawmakers listened in silence till the darkness began to fade and the sky grew bright again.

1. Based on this story, how would you describe Abraham Davenport's personality?

2. How are the other people at the statehouse different from Abraham Davenport?

3. Which of these lines from the passage shows a character expressing an opinion?

    A. "What is the matter?"
    B. "This is the last great day!"
    C. "I do not know whether the end of the world has come or not..."
    D. "When the darkness came, they began to be alarmed."

4. Why does Abraham Davenport propose the law to help poor fisherman?

    A. To show that people should continue living as normal, even though confusing things were happening outside
    B. To show people that even very poor people are important to a successful society
    C. To show people he wasn't scared of the dark
    D. To show people that the same things are important in the darkness that are important in the light

5. How does this story show that opinion can get out of control when people don't have enough facts?

WEEK 7 DAY 2

 Directions:

Read each sentence, then write on the line below whether it is **fact** or **opinion**. Once you've done that, circle the words in the sentence that helped you choose your answer.

1. Nobody likes video games with bad graphics because they are boring to look at.

    ~~~~~~~~~~~~~~~~~~~~~~~~~~~~~~~~~~~~

2. Christine knits the most beautiful scarves I've seen in my life.

    ~~~~~~~~~~~~~~~~~~~~~~~~~~~~~~~~~~~~

3. Clean drinking water is crucial to public health because our bodies need hydration and contaminants in water can be extremely dangerous.

    ~~~~~~~~~~~~~~~~~~~~~~~~~~~~~~~~~~~~

4. World War II occurred between 1939 and 1945, with battles taking place in both Europe and the Pacific.

    ~~~~~~~~~~~~~~~~~~~~~~~~~~~~~~~~~~~~

5. My dad's car is much cooler than my mom's because it's a red sports car.

    ~~~~~~~~~~~~~~~~~~~~~~~~~~~~~~~~~~~~

FITNESS

Please be aware of your environment and be safe at all times. If you cannot do an exercise, just try your best.

Repeat these **exercises 3 ROUNDS**

1 - Squats:
5 times.
Note: imagine you are trying to sit on a chair.

2 - Side Bending:
5 times to each side. Note: try to touch your feet.

3 - Tree Pose:
Stay as long as possible.
Note: do the same with the other leg.

Word problems dealing with mass and volume

1. Franny bought 3 pounds of sweets. James bought 51 ounces of sweets. Who bought more sweets? Prove your answer.

   A. Franny bought more because she bought pounds and pounds is greater than ounces.

   B. They bought the same amount because 3 pounds = 51 ounces.

   C. James bought more because 3 pounds is 48 ounces and James bought 51 ounces of sweets.

   D. James bought more because 51 > 3.

2. A coffee machine can store 8 liters of coffee. How much coffee can it store in mL?

   A. 8 mL
   B. 80 mL
   C. 800 mL
   D. 8,000 mL

3. The weight of 4 cats is shown below.

Cats	Pounds
1	9
2	6
3	15
4	10

   If all 4 cats were placed on a scale, how much would the scale read, in ounces?

   A. 640 oz
   B. 320 oz
   C. 76 oz
   D. 1,820 oz

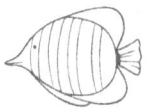

4. Alexander caught 3 fishes that were 2 kg and 200 g, 2 kg and 400 g, 3 kg and 150 g in weight. How many kilograms did the three fishes weigh together?

   Answer _____

5. A farmer wanted to determine the weight of a hen. Which of the following is the best estimate for the weight of a hen?

   A. 3 kilograms
   B. 100 grams
   C. 30 centimeters
   D. 30 decimeters

Temperature (Celcius) °

1. What is the temperature?

   A. 0°
   B. 5°
   C. 10°
   D. 15°

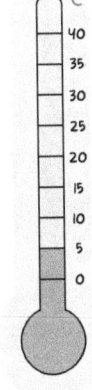

2. On Monday morning the temperature was 23° Celsius. During the night, the temperature dropped 9° Celsius. What was the temperature at night?

   A. 9° C
   B. 12° C
   C. 14° C
   D. 32° C

3. What is the difference between the measurements on the first and the second thermometer?

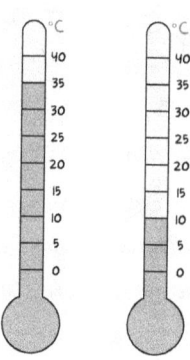

Answer _____

4. What is the temperature?

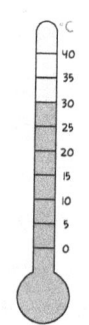

Answer _____

5. On a hot summer day the temperature was 32° Celsius. Later in the evening, the temperature rose 3.4° Celsius. What was the temperature in the evening?

A. 28.6° C
B. 35.4° C
C. 37.4° C
D. 66° C

6. What is the difference between the two measurements represented on the thermometers below?

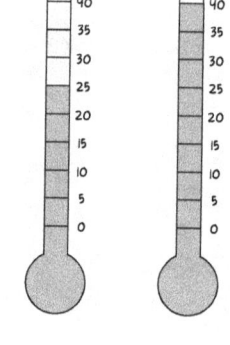

Answer _____

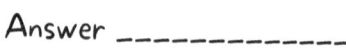

FITNESS

Please be aware of your environment and be safe at all times. If you cannot do an exercise, just try your best.

Repeat these **exercises 3 ROUNDS**

1 - Bend forward: 10 times.
Note: try to touch your feet. Make sure to keep your back straight and if needed you can bend your knees.

2 - Lunges: 3 times to each leg.
Note: Use your body weight or books as weight to do leg lunges.

3 - Plank: 6 sec.

4 - Abs: 10 times

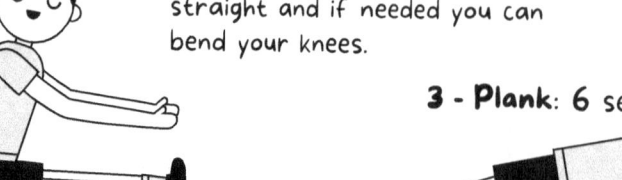
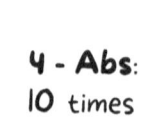

WEEK 7 DAY 4  MATH

Temperature (Celcius) °

1. On Monday morning the temperature was 21° C. Five hours later, the temperature dropped 3° C. By nighttime, the temperature rose 4° C. What was the temperature at nighttime?

    A. 9° C
    B. 14° C
    C. 22° C
    D. 28° C

2. On Thursday morning the temperature was 31° C. Six hours later, the temperature dropped 6° C. By nighttime, the temperature dropped another 2° C. What was the temperature at nighttime?

    A. 23° C
    B. 25° C
    C. 37° C
    D. 39° C

3. Which tool would you use to find out how warm the tea is in a cup?

    A. Measuring cup
    B. Thermometer
    C. Teaspoon
    D. Ruler

4. What is the difference between the temperature measured in thermometer 4 and 3?

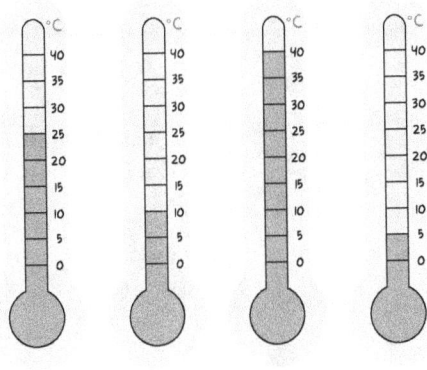

1   2   3   4

A. 10° C
B. 20° C
C. 30° C
D. 35° C

5. The temperature falls from 12° C to -1° C. How many degrees does the temperature fall?

    A. 2° C
    B. 9° C
    C. 13° C
    D. 15° C

Rewriting fractions as decimals

1. Find the fraction that is equivalent to 0.2.

    A. $\frac{2}{10}$

    B. $\frac{1}{2}$

    C. $\frac{20}{10}$

    D. $\frac{1}{4}$

2. What is $\frac{6}{10}$ rewritten as a decimal?

    A. 6.0
    B. 0.6
    C. 6.6
    D. 0.06

3. Which number sentence is true?

    A. $\frac{5}{10}$ = 0.2

    B. $\frac{1}{3}$ = 0.3

    C. $\frac{6}{10}$ = 6.1

    D. $\frac{4}{10}$ = 0.4

4. Convert the fraction $\frac{8}{10}$ into a decimal.

    A. 8.0
    B. 0.8
    C. 8.8
    D. 88

5. How can $\frac{1}{2}$ be written as a decimal?

    A. 0.2
    B. 2.2
    C. 0.5
    D. 2.0

6. Write a decimal that is equivalent to $\frac{3}{10}$.

    Answer _____

7. Convert the fraction $\frac{2}{4}$ into a decimal.

    Answer _____

8. The rope is half a meter in length. What is its length as a decimal?

    Answer _____

9. Convert the fraction $\frac{9}{10}$ into a decimal.

    Answer _____

10. Write a quarter of a meter as a decimal. Hint: What is the value of a quarter when we think about money?

    Answer _____

FITNESS

Please be aware of your environment and be safe at all times. If you cannot do an exercise, just try your best.

Repeat these **exercises 3 ROUNDS**

1 - High Plank: 6 sec.

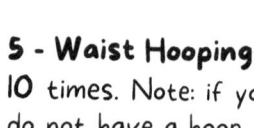

5 - Waist Hooping: 10 times. Note: if you do not have a hoop, pretend you have an imaginary hoop and rotate your hips 10 times.

2 - Chair: 10 sec. Note: sit on an imaginary chair, keep your back straight.

4 - Abs: 10 times

3 - Side Bending: 5 times to each side. Note: try to touch your feet.

WEEK 7 DAY 5  MATH

Various Real World Word Problems

1. David ran 855 yards. Jane ran 645 yards. What distance did they run altogether?

   A. 1,100 yd
   B. 1,200 yd
   C. 1,300 yd
   D. 1,500 yd

2. Rihanna had 8 days to complete her essay. How many hours did she have?

   A. 182 hours
   B. 192 hours
   C. 202 hours
   D. 212 hours

3. The apple tree had 6 times as many fruits as the peach tree. The peach tree had 45 fruits. How many fruits did the apple tree have?

   A. 250
   B. 260
   C. 270
   D. 280

4. Below is a chart showing the time it took some students to run a mile.

Student	Time (minutes)
Mason	10
Kyle	9
Sharon	12

   A. How much faster did Kyle run the mile than Sharon?

   Answer _____

   B. How much slower (in minutes) was Mason than Kyle?

   Answer _____

5. Helen baked biscuits and placed them in boxes that could contain 9 biscuits each. If she baked 180 biscuits, how many boxes did she use?

   A. 12
   B. 15
   C. 20
   D. 27

6. Robbin got to the gym at 4:15 p.m. She left the gym at 5:40 p.m. How long was she at the gym?

   Answer _____

7. Mark earns $835 per week, and Jessica earns $915 per week. How much do they earn in total per week?

   A. $1,750
   B. $1,450
   C. $1,950
   D. $1,650

8. Mary swims 7 laps every day. If she has swam 119 laps so far this month, how many days out of this month did she swim?

   A. 15 days
   B. 17 days
   C. 19 days
   D. 13 days

9. On Tuesday, Saul earned $113 selling blueberry pies. On Saturday, he earned $206 selling the pies. He spent $15 on buying flour and $26 buying sugar.

   A. How much money did Saul earn on these two days not including his expenses?

   Answer _____

   B. What was Saul's pure profit after his expenses?

   Answer _____

10. The perimeter of Isabella's square carpet is **36** feet. Help Isabella to find the area of her carpet.

    A. **76** sq ft
    B. **79** sq ft
    C. **81** sq ft
    D. **86** sq ft

11. Claire purchased a square pillow that has a perimeter of **108** inches. What is the length of one side of the pillow?

    A. **27** in
    B. **29** in
    C. **32** in
    D. **33** in

12. Lilly recorded the amount of problems she solved each week before the test. If this pattern continues, how many problems will she solve on Week **8**?

Week 1	Week 2	Week 3	Week 4	Week 5
9	12	15	18	21

    A. 27
    B. 28
    C. 29
    D. 30

13. Alex set the thermostat in her house to **22°C**, which was **8°** warmer than the temperature outside. What was the temperature outside?

    Answer _____

YOGA

Please be aware of your environment and be safe at all times. If you cannot do an exercise, just try your best.

1 - Down Dog: 10 sec.

2 - Bend Down: 10 sec.

3 - Chair: 10 sec.

4 - Child Pose: 20 sec.

5 - Shavasana: as long as you can. Note: think of happy moments and relax your mind.

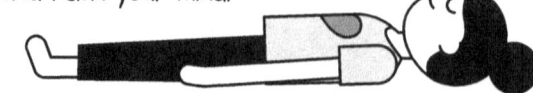

WEEK 7 DAY 6  EXPERIMENT

Observing Static Charge Using Your Body

Over the last two weeks, we've seen how **magnetic charge** can help move or lift objects. This week, we're going to look at a different kind of **charge**: static electricity. Static is created when one **motion** builds up an **electrical** charge.

Materials:

- An inflated balloon (it can be inflated with oxygen or helium - either is fine)
- A plastic comb
- A mirror
- Note paper

Procedure:

1. Blow up the balloon and tie it closed, or get an adult to do it

2. Stand in front of the mirror and **rub the inflated balloon quickly back-and-forth across your hair** for 10 to 15 seconds to build an electrical charge.

3. Slowly lift the away from the top of your head and **observe what happens to your hair.** Move the balloon around your head to see what happens, and take note of how far you can move the balloon before it stops controlling your hair. If you want to experiment further, you can rub the balloon against your hair again to charge it back up. (**NOTE**: If you have a buzz cut or very short hair, you may want to test this on someone else in your family to observe the results better.)

4. Take 10 minutes to let the charge die down, then write down what you observed on your note paper.

5. Stand in front of the mirror again, this time with the plastic comb, and **comb your dry hair straight back, very quickly, going only one direction.** After about 15 seconds of rapid combing, lift the comb just above the front of your hair, and see what happens. Make note of this on your note sheet.

6. Take **5** more minutes to let the charge die down and answer the two questions below.

7. If you have hair on your arms or legs, you can charge the balloon up on your head one more time and see if you can use it to move your arm or leg hairs. Notice how that hair responds differently than the longer hair on top of your head.

135

Follow-Up Questions:

1. Based on what you saw today and what you saw over the last two weeks, how are **magnetism** and **static electricity** similar?

2. How were the effects of the **balloon** and the **comb** different?

Please be aware of your environment and be safe at all times. If you cannot do an exercise, just try your best.

1 - Tree Pose: Stay as long as possible. Note: do on one leg then on another.

2 - Down Dog: 10 sec.

3 - Stretching: Stay as long as possible. Note: do on one leg then on another.

4 - Lower Plank: 6 sec. Note: Keep your back straight and body tight.

5 -Book Pose: 6 sec. Note: Keep your core tight. Legs should be across from your eyes.

6 - Shavasana: 5 min. Note: this pose is very important and provides you with long term benefits. Try not to skip this. Close your eyes and imagine who you want to be and what your goals are! Always think happy thoughts.

WEEK 7 DAY 7  MAZE

Task: Michelle is getting wet from the rain. Help her find the way through the maze so she can meet her friend Elijah who has an umbrella! Color in the pathway.

Superb!
This week we will learn about nouns, practice real-life math word problems, and learn about static charge. Let's go :)

WEEK 8

It's an octopus!
Did you know an octopus has three hearts? Two of the hearts are responsible for pumping the blood to the gills, and the third heart circulates the blood around the body.

WEEK 8 DAY 1  OVERVIEW OF ENGLISH CONCEPTS NOUNS

Now that you're experienced at reading and writing sentences, it's time to take your understanding of how words work to a new level! Different kinds of words do different jobs in sentences. We call those different types of words the **parts of speech**. The four most basic parts of speech that we use to create sentences are nouns, verbs, adjectives, and adverbs. We'll start by talking about **nouns**! A noun is a word that represents a person, place, or thing.

 Key Terms

Noun: A word that represents a person, place, or thing

 For Example...

A noun that represents a **person** could take the form of someone's **name**, a **job** description, or some other word that describes who or what they are.

Examples of Nouns that Represent People:		
Person	Brother	Dancer
Mr. Fernandez	Artist	Ms. Schwarz
Student	Nurse	Mom
Athlete	Francine	Goalie

In the sentence:

🐚 <u>Mr. James</u> always eats a sandwich for lunch at the cafeteria.

🐚 My <u>Aunt Kelly</u> was a great <u>swimmer</u> on the Stanford University team.

A noun that represents a **place** could take the form of a specific place's **name**, or it might just be a general description of the place.

Examples of Nouns that Represent Places:		
New York	Downtown	Beach
Bus Stop	Theme Park	Europe
Home	Bus Stop	California
Bedroom	City	Country

In the sentence:

🐚 Mr. James always eats a sandwich for lunch at the <u>cafeteria.</u>

🐚 My Aunt Kelly was a great swimmer on the <u>Stanford University</u> team.

A noun that represents a thing could take the form of a specific object's name (like a product with a brand name), or it might just be a word that represents a certain item or idea...

Examples of Nouns that Represent Things:		
Finger	Plate	Scissors
Math	Computer	Phone
Map	Ketchup	Baseball
Dog	Shoe	Pencil

In the sentence:

🐚 Mr. James always eats a <u>sandwich</u> for <u>lunch</u> at the cafeteria.

🐚 My Aunt Kelly was a great swimmer on the Stanford University <u>team</u>.

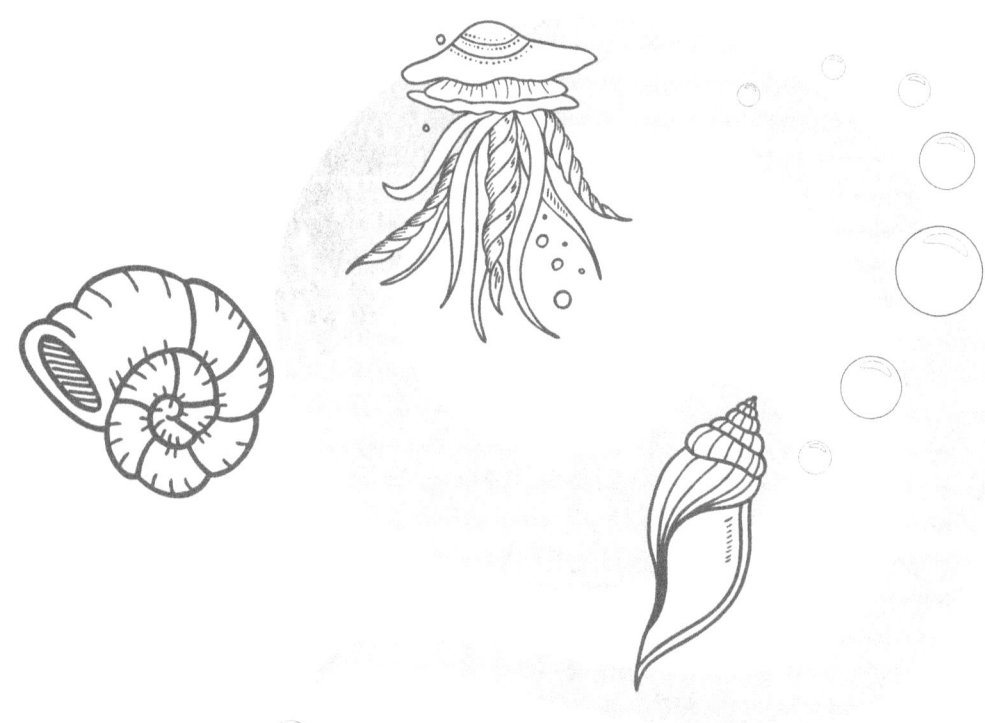

The Mule and the Lapdog
By Aesop

A MAN had a mule, and a Maltese Lapdog, a very great beauty. The mule was left in a stable and had plenty of oats and hay to eat, just as any other mule would. The Lapdog knew many tricks and was a great favorite with his master, who often played with him and seldom went out to dine without bringing him home some tidbit to eat.

The mule, on the contrary, had much work to do in grinding the corn-mill and in carrying wood from the forest or burdens from the farm. He often lamented his own hard fate and contrasted it with the luxury and idleness of the Lapdog, till at last one day he broke his cords and halter, and galloped into his master's house, kicking up his heels without measure, and frisking and fawning as well as he could. He next tried to jump about his master as he had seen the Lapdog do, but he broke the table and smashed all the dishes upon it to atoms. He then attempted to lick his master, and jumped upon his back.

The servants, hearing the strange hubbub and perceiving the danger of their master, quickly relieved him, and drove out the mule to his stable with kicks and clubs and cuffs. The mule, as he returned to his stall beaten nearly to death, thus lamented: "I have brought it all on myself! Why could I not have been contented to labor with my companions, and not wish to be idle all the day like that useless little Lapdog!"

1. What does the mule want at the beginning of the story?

2. Why is the mule jealous of the lapdog?

3. Which of these words from the first paragraph of the story is not a noun?

   A. Mule
   B. Stable
   C. Lapdog
   D. Eat

4. Why do the master's servants attack the mule when it tries to act like the lapdog?

   A. They are angry that the mule is not acting like the correct animal
   B. They are scared that he might injure or kill his master
   C. They are concerned the mule will eat all the food
   D. They are scared because they've never seen a mule before

5. Do you agree with the mule that he should've been happy to work with the other mules, rather than trying to live like a pet? Why or why not?

WEEK 8 DAY 1 ACTIVITIES NOUNS

 Directions:

Circle or underline the nouns in the following sentences. For each noun you find, write whether it represents a **person, place, or thing** either above or below it.

1. Our family's cat is always trying to catch mice in the basement.

2. Mr. Pew had to call a tow truck because he locked his keys in the trunk of the car.

3. The brilliant artist spent hours mixing up different colors in his studio before he started the painting.

4. The old train rattled along the tracks between New York and Philadelphia, which was a very bumpy ride for passengers.

5. In baseball, the catcher is one of the most important people in the entire stadium.

FITNESS

Please be aware of your environment and be safe at all times. If you cannot do an exercise, just try your best.

Repeat these
exercises
3 ROUNDS

1 - Abs:
3 times

2 - Lunges:
2 times to each leg.
Note: Use your body weight or books as weight to do leg lunges.

3 - Lunges:
3 times to each leg.
Note: Use your body weight or books as weight to do leg lunges.

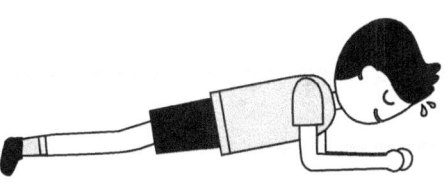

5 - Plank: 6 sec.

4 - Run: 50m
Note: Run **25** meters to one side and **25** meters back to the starting position.

The Boy and the Wolf
By James Baldwin

In France there once lived a famous man who was known as the Marquis de Lafayette. When he was a little boy his mother called him Gilbert.

Gilbert de Lafayette's father and grandfather and great-grandfather had all been brave and noble men. He was very proud to think of this, and he wished that he might grow up to be like them.

His home was in the country not far from a great forest. Often, when he was a little lad, he took long walks among the trees with his mother.

"Mother," he would say, "do not be afraid. I am with you, and I will not let anything hurt you."

One day word came that a savage wolf had been seen in the forest. Men said that it was a very large wolf and that it had killed some of the farmers' sheep.

"How I should like to meet that wolf," said little Gilbert.

He was only seven years old, but now all his thoughts were about the savage beast that was in the forest.

"Shall we take a walk this morning?" asked his mother.

"Oh, yes!" said Gilbert. "Perhaps we may see that wolf among the trees.

But don't be afraid."

His mother smiled, for she felt quite sure that there was no danger.

They did not go far into the woods. The mother sat down in the shade of a tree and began to read in a new book which she had bought the day before. The boy played on the grass nearby.

The sun was warm. The bees were buzzing among the flowers. The small birds were singing softly. Gilbert looked up from his play and saw that his mother was very deeply interested in her book.

"Now for the wolf!" he said to himself.

He walked quickly, but very quietly, down the pathway into the darker woods. He looked eagerly around, but saw only a squirrel frisking among the trees and a rabbit hopping across the road.

Soon he came to a wilder place. There the bushes were very close together and the pathway came to an end. He pushed the bushes aside and went a little farther. How still everything was!

He could see a green open space just beyond; and then the woods seemed to be thicker and darker. "This is just the place for that wolf," he thought.

1. What kind of family does it seem like Gilbert de Lafayette comes from?

2. How would you describe the character of Gilbert's mother? What parts of the story helped you understand what she was like?

3. Which of these words from the second paragraph is not a noun?

   A. Gilbert
   B. Great-grandfather
   C. Men
   D. Proud

4. Whose plan is it to enter the woods? Why do they want to go?

   A. It is Gilbert's plan. He wants to go to catch the wolf.
   B. It is Gilbert's plan. He is bored and wants to play outside.
   C. It is Gilbert's mother's plan. She wants to go and catch the wolf.
   D. It is Gilbert's mother's plan. She believes the woods are safe and wants Gilbert to get out of the house.

5. Why do you think young Gilbert is so fascinated by the idea of the wolf? Which details from the text helped you come up with your answer?

 Directions:

Each group of words contains three nouns and two words that are not nouns. Circle or underline the words in each group that are not nouns.

1. SQUIRREL	MIKE	READ	CHEESE	CREEPY
2. WINTER	TENNESSEE	INTO	STADIUM	FRAMED
3. HAPPY	HOLE	INTERNET	SAD	REFRIGERATOR
4. ARMS	CLASSROOM	SQUID	RIDICULOUS	THROW
5. CONFUSING	STRICT	PIANO	CANADA	APPLE

Please be aware of your environment and be safe at all times. If you cannot do an exercise, just try your best.

Repeat these **exercises 3 ROUNDS**

3 - Side Bending: 5 times to each side. Note: try to touch your feet.

4 - Abs: 10 times

2 - Squats: 5 times. Note: imagine you are trying to sit on a chair.

5 - Tree Pose: Stay as long as possible. Note: do the same with the other leg.

1 - High Plank: 6 sec.

WEEK 8 DAY 3  MATH

Various Real World Word Problems

1. The instructions to cook a stew say to set the oven at 160°C. If Mrs. Sanchez set her oven 12° cooler than the instructions said, what temperature did she set her oven to?

   Answer _____

2. Mr. Cooper has a pool in the shape of a rectangle. How many sides will the pool have?

   Answer _____

3. Sonora cut a piece of fabric into a shape with 5 sides. What is the name of this shape?

   Answer _____

4. Vincent created a chart showing how many points he had at the end of each level of a computer game. How would you determine the points he would have at the end of level 9?

Levels	2	3	4	5	6
Points	12	18	24	30	36

   A. Add 6 to 9
   B. Add 6 to 12
   C. Multiply 12 by 9
   D. Multiply 6 by 9

5. Garry walked $\frac{2}{5}$ of a mile on Monday and another $\frac{2}{5}$ of a mile on Tuesday. What was the total distance he walked?

   Answer _____

6. Iren's class is going to visit a museum. If each car can hold five people and there are fourteen students and 9 adults going, how many cars will they need?

   A. 3 cars
   B. 4 cars
   C. 5 cars
   D. 6 cars

7. Natalie had a piece of ribbon that measured $\frac{6}{8}$ yards in length. If she cut $\frac{2}{8}$ yards of the ribbon, what is the new length of the ribbon?

   Answer _____

8. There are 365 days in one year. How many days are in 11 years?

   Answer _____

9. A certain farm packs peaches in boxes that hold 10 each. Today the farm packed 4,820 peaches. How many boxes did they use to pack the peaches?

   Answer _____

10. An outside garbage can weighs **256** oz. A kitchen garbage can weighs **189** oz. Which weighs more and by how much?

    Answer _____

11. Theatre A seated **345** people and Theatre B seated **653** people. Which theatre sat more people and by how much more?

    Answer _____

12. Vicky was making herself some hot chocolate. Did she most likely use half a cup of milk or half a gallon of milk? Explain your reasoning.

    Answer _____

13. Gigi bought a bottle of juice. What seems more likely? The juice was **450** milliliters or the juice was **450** liters? Explain your reasoning.

    Answer _____

14. Martha purchased carrots to use in a recipe to cook for dinner for her family of four. What seems more reasonable, Martha purchased **3** pounds of carrots or **3** ounces of carrots?

    Answer _____

15. Amy eats cereal in the morning. Does she most likely eat **50** grams or **5** kilograms of cereal?

    Answer _____

FITNESS

Please be aware of your environment and be safe at all times. If you cannot do an exercise, just try your best.

Repeat these **exercises 3 ROUNDS**

1 - Bend forward: 10 times. Note: try to touch your feet. Make sure to keep your back straight and if needed you can bend your knees.

2 - Lunges: 3 times to each leg. Note: Use your body weight or books as weight to do leg lunges.

3 - Plank: 6 sec.

4 - Abs: 10 times

WEEK 8 DAY 4  MATH

Various Real World Word Problems

The table below show the number of essays students wrote each month. Use the data to answer questions 1 - 2.

Months	Essays written per month by students
September	4
October	7
November	9
December	6

1. How many more essays were written by students in November than in September?

   A. 3
   B. 2
   C. 5
   D. 4

2. How many essays did students write in the month of October and December in total?

   Answer _____

3. Fred drew an angle of 80°. What type of angle is it?

   A. Acute
   B. Obtuse
   C. Right
   D. None of the above

4. What type of angles are in the rectangular kitchen? What is each angle measure?

   Answer _____

5. Nina baked 37 pies on Wednesday, and 69 pies on Friday. How many pies did she bake in total?

   Answer _____

A pizza cafe kept track of the different toppings they sold in a week. They recorded the results in the bar graph below. Use the graph to answer questions 6 - 7.

Most Sold Pizza Toppings

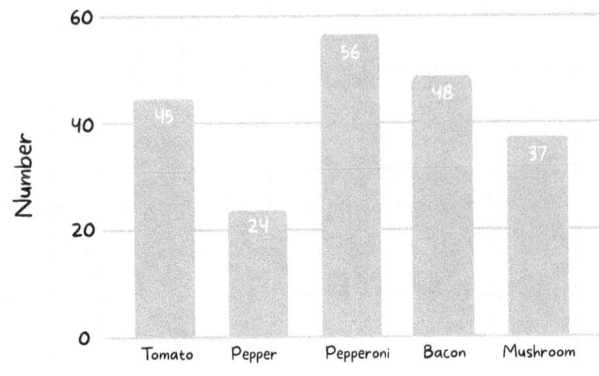

6. Which is the most popular topping?

   Answer _____

7. How many customers have chosen tomato or pepperoni toppings?

   Answer _____

8. Jenny cut a piece of paper that measured 8 centimeters wide and 14 centimeters long. What is the perimeter of the paper she cut out?

   A. 112 cm
   B. 44 cm
   C. 68 cm
   D. 22 cm

9. A backyard has a length of 16 meters and a total area of 144 square meters. What is the width of the backyard?

   A. 5
   B. 7
   C. 8
   D. 9

10. Liam was buying pens of different colors. He bought 17 pens at the store and he bought 19 blue pens online. How many pens did he buy in total?

    Answer _____

11. Billy bought 16 baseballs at the sports store. If each baseball cost $8 and he paid with 3 fifty dollar bills, how much change should he get back?

    A. $22
    B. $24
    C. $28
    D. $32

12. Denise spent 3 hours and 21 minutes playing computer games. If she stopped to eat dinner at 7:40 pm, what time did she start playing her computer games?

    Answer _____

FITNESS

Please be aware of your environment and be safe at all times. If you cannot do an exercise, just try your best.

Repeat these exercises **3 ROUNDS**

1 - High Plank: 6 sec.

2 - Chair: 10 sec. Note: sit on an imaginary chair, keep your back straight.

3 - Waist Hooping: 10 times. Note: if you do not have a hoop, pretend you have an imaginary hoop and rotate your hips 10 times.

4 - Abs: 10 times

Placing fractions on a number line

1. Which fraction is missing from the number line?

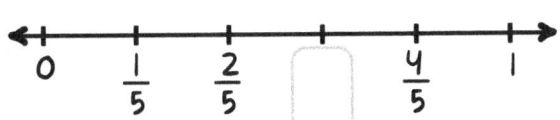

Answer _____

2. Which fraction represents one equal part of this number line?

A. $\dfrac{1}{4}$

B. $\dfrac{1}{8}$

C. $\dfrac{1}{9}$

D. $\dfrac{1}{10}$

3. Find the missing fraction on the number line.

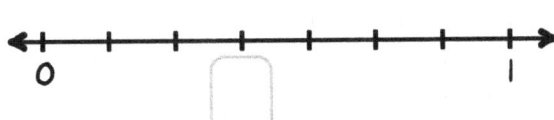

A. $\dfrac{3}{5}$

B. $\dfrac{3}{7}$

C. $\dfrac{3}{6}$

D. $\dfrac{1}{7}$

4. Where is the point on the number line?

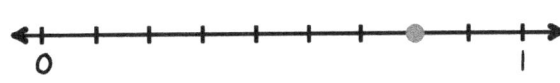

A. $\dfrac{1}{9}$

B. $\dfrac{2}{9}$

C. $\dfrac{7}{9}$

D. $\dfrac{8}{9}$

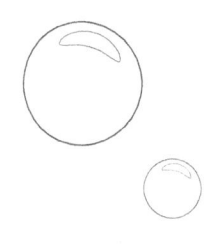

5. Find the value of k.

Answer _____

6. Which place on the number line is equal to the shaded part of the fraction represented in the picture below?

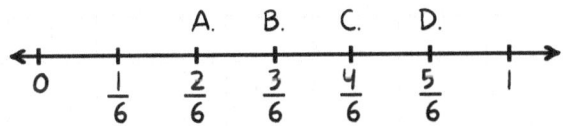

A. $\dfrac{2}{6}$

B. $\dfrac{3}{6}$

C. $\dfrac{4}{6}$

D. $\dfrac{5}{6}$

7. Find the missing fractions on the number line.

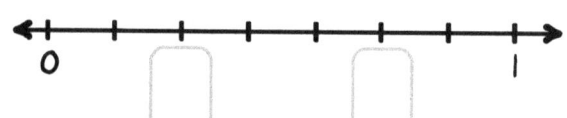

A. $\frac{2}{6}$ and $\frac{5}{6}$

B. $\frac{2}{6}$ and $\frac{4}{6}$

C. $\frac{2}{7}$ and $\frac{4}{6}$

D. $\frac{2}{7}$ and $\frac{5}{7}$

8. What fractions do the letters K and L represent on the number line?

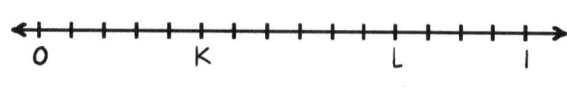

Answer _____

9. Draw the dot at $\frac{4}{10}$ on the number line.

Answer

10. Which place on the number line is equal to the fraction represented in the picture below?

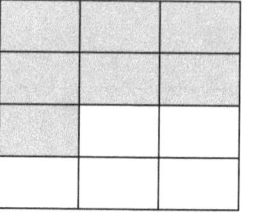

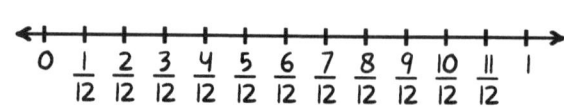

Answer _____

YOGA

Please be aware of your environment and be safe at all times. If you cannot do an exercise, just try your best.

1 - Down Dog: 10 sec.

2 - Bend Down: 10 sec.

3 - Chair: 10 sec.

4 - Child Pose: 20 sec.

5 - Shavasana: as long as you can. Note: think of happy moments and relax your mind.

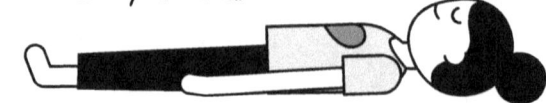

WEEK 8 DAY 6  EXPERIMENT

Using a Static Charge to Move Objects

Last week, we used a **balloon** and a **comb** to build up a static charge that we could observe using our bodies. Now we'll see how static can influence the **movement** of other objects.

Materials:

- A plastic comb
- A kitchen or bathroom sink
- Two Styrofoam plates (ideally, one big one and one small one)
- A washcloth or small towel
- Note paper

Procedure:

1. First, set the plates and towel aside and **comb your hair quickly, in one direction**, over and over for **30** seconds like you did last week to build up static electricity. Your hair needs to be dry for this to work.

2. Turn on the sink, but not to full blast. You want there to be **a small, consistent stream of water** (not just drips).

3. Hold the comb vertically (straight up and down) and **move it close to the stream of water. Observe what happens when the charged-up comb comes near** the stream of water. (If nothing happens, dry off the comb, comb your hair quickly for a little longer, and try again.)

4. Turn off the sink and set the comb aside. Take the two Styrofoam plates and the washcloth to a **clean, dry**, and **flat surface**, like a counter or tabletop.

5. Put one of the Styrofoam plates (the bigger one, if you have both sizes) **face-down on the counter**.

6. Using the washcloth or small towel, **rub the bottom side of the second (small) Styrofoam plate aggressively for several seconds**. This is generating a static charge, just like when you combed your hair.

7. **Try to place the small plate on top of the large plate**, bottom side to bottom side. Observe what happens.

8. Pick the small plate back up and hold it in one hand. Open your other hand flat and hold it about 6-12 inches above the large plate with your palm down. Then, using your other hand, hold the small plate between your palm and the big plate and let go. Observe what happens and write it down on your note sheet.

WEEK 8 DAY 6  EXPERIMENT

Follow-Up Questions:

1. Why were combing your hair and rubbing the Styrofoam plate with the cloth such important parts of both processes?

2. Based on what you've seen over the last 4 weeks, how can a **charge** (like magnetism or static electricity) be useful for people?

YOGA

Please be aware of your environment and be safe at all times. If you cannot do an exercise, just try your best.

1 - Tree Pose: Stay as long as possible. Note: do on one leg then on another.

2 - Down Dog: 10 sec.

3 - Stretching: Stay as long as possible. Note: do on one leg then on another.

4 - Lower Plank: 6 sec. Note: Keep your back straight and body tight.

5 - Book Pose: 6 sec. Note: Keep your core tight. Legs should be across from your eyes.

6 - Shavasana: 5 min. Note: this pose is very important and provides you with long term benefits. Try not to skip this. Close your eyes and imagine who you want to be and what your goals are! Always think happy thoughts.

WEEK 8 DAY 7 CROSSWORD

Task: Take a look at the eight pictures below and fill out the crossword puzzle.

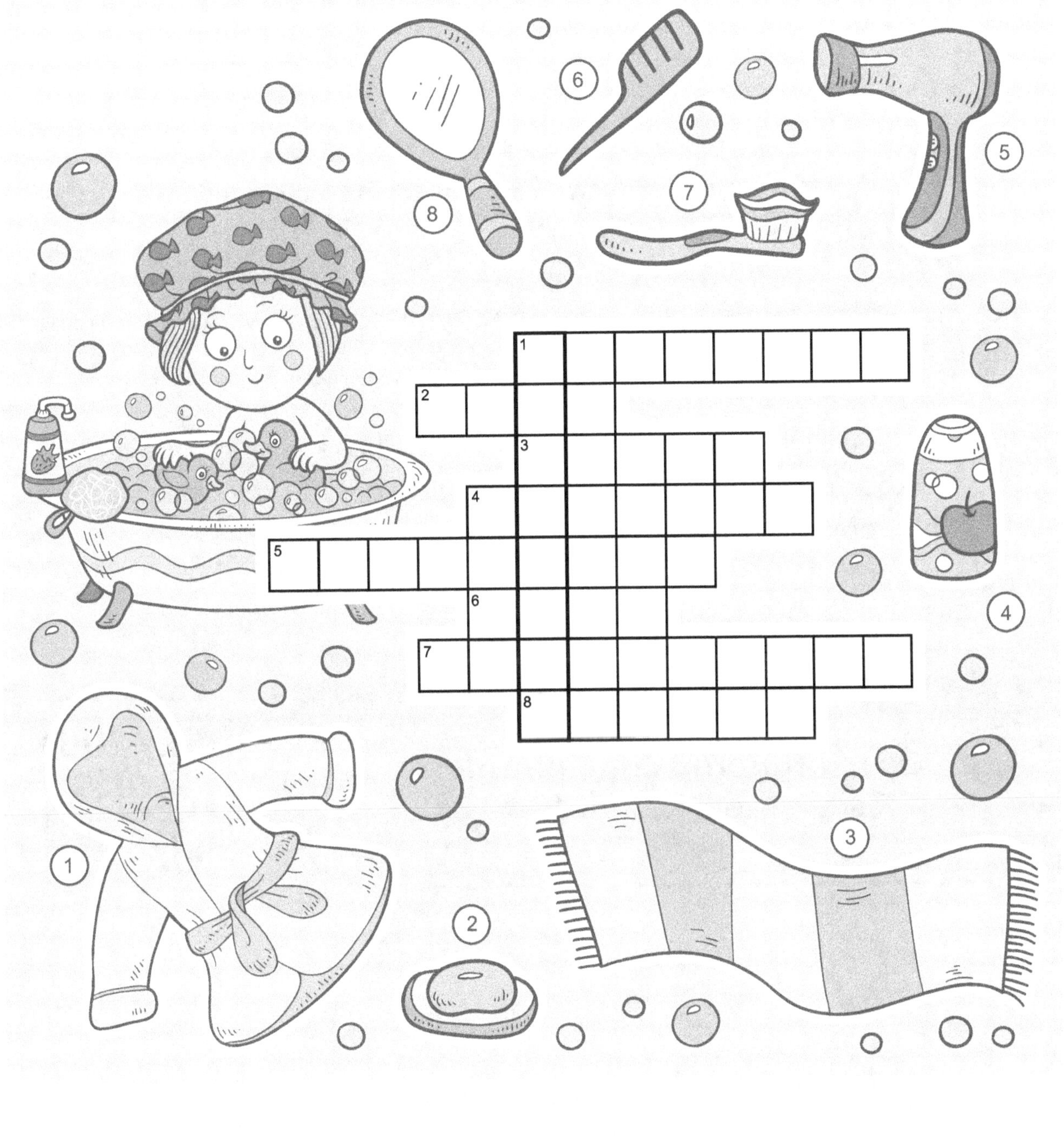

Answer Sheets

To see the answer key to the entire workbook, you can easily download the answer key from our website!

*Due to the high request from parents and teachers, we have removed the answer key from the workbook so you do not need to rip out the answer key while students work on the workbook.

Go to **argoprep.com/summer4**
OR scan the QR Code:

Kids Summer Academy by ArgoPrep:
Grade 8-9

Kids Summer Academy by ArgoPrep:
Grade 5-6

Kids Summer Academy by ArgoPrep:
Grade 4-5

Kids Summer Academy by ArgoPrep:
Grade 6-7

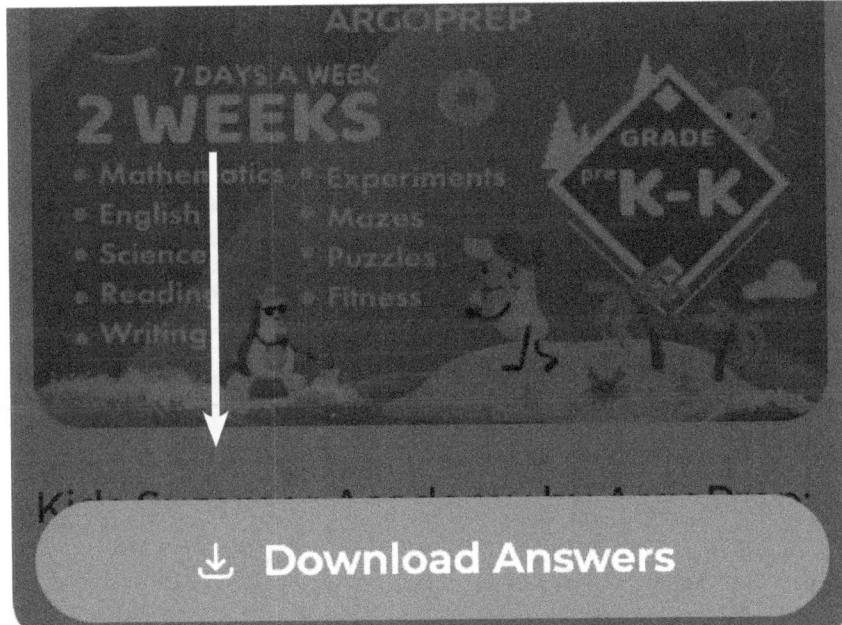

Kids Summer
Grade 8-9

www.ingramcontent.com/pod-product-compliance
Lightning Source LLC
Chambersburg PA
CBHW081330120626
46546CB00011B/3283